THE
POLITICAL
SPECTRUM

Opposing Viewpoints

THE POLITICAL SPECTRUM

Opposing Viewpoints

David L. Bender
Bruno Leone

OPPOSING VIEWPOINTS SERIES

Greenhaven Press

577 SHOREVIEW PARK ROAD
ST. PAUL, MINNESOTA 55112

© Copyright 1981 by Greenhaven Press, Inc.

ISBN 0-89908-300-5
ISBN 0-89908-325-0

CONGRESS SHALL MAKE NO LAW... ABRIDGING THE FREEDOM OF SPEECH, OR OF THE PRESS

first amendment to the U.S. Constitution

The basic foundation of our democracy is the first amendment guarantee of freedom of expression. The OPPOSING VIEWPOINTS SERIES is dedicated to the concept of this basic freedom and the idea that it is more important to practice it than to enshrine it.

TABLE OF CONTENTS   Page

The Opposing Viewpoints Series   9

The Political Animal   15

Chapter 1: WHAT IS THE POLITICAL SPECTRUM?

  1. **The Spectrum as a Straight Line**   18
     David L. Bender

  2. **The Spectrum as a Diamond**   21
     Ferdinand V. Solara

  3. **A Conservative Views the Spectrum**   23
     George A. Reimann

  4. **A Liberal Views the Spectrum**   28
     Henry Steele Commager

  5. **The Spectrum Keeps Changing**   33
     Joseph C. Harsch

Chapter 2: WHAT IS LIBERALISM?

  1. **What Liberalism Is**   41
     David Sidorsky

  2. **America Is Better for Liberalism**   44
     Henry Fairlie

  3. **America Is Worse for Liberalism**   49
     Ben Stein

  4. **A Liberal Looks at the Eighties**   55
     Paul E. Tsongas

  5. **A Conservative Looks at the Eighties**   60
     Jack Kemp

Chapter 3: WHAT IS CONSERVATISM?

  1. **What Conservatism Is**   71
     Jay A. Sigler

  2. **The Conservative View of Freedom**   75
     Milton Friedman

  3. **The Liberal View of Freedom**   80
     Milton Viorst

  4. **What Is Neo-Conservatism?**   84
     Irving Kristol

  5. **A Critique of Neo-Conservatism**   89
     Isidore Silver

Chapter 4: WHAT IS EXTREMISM?

1. **What Extremism Is**   99
   David L. Bender and Bruno Leone

2. **Socialism in America – The Political Left**   105
   Harold Freeman

3. **"I Am a Reactionary" – The Political Right**   109
   Patricia Young

4. **What Libertarianism Is**   115
   John Hospers

5. **A Conservative Reply to Libertarianism**   122
   Ernest van den Haag

6. **A Liberal Reply to Libertarianism**   127
   James W. Woelfel

Index of Liberal Publications   66

Index of Conservative Publications   93

Index of Far Right and Far Left Publications   132

Helpful Periodical Articles   138

Index   141

Discussion Activities
1. **Understanding Stereotypes**   36
2. **Revolution and Change**   68
3. **Distinguishing Between Fact and Opinion**   95
4. **Distinguishing Between Bias and Reason**   113
5. **Labeling Individuals and Organizations**   136

the Opposing viewpoints series

THE IMPORTANCE OF EXAMINING
OPPOSING VIEWPOINTS

The purpose of this book, and the Opposing Viewpoints Series as a whole, is to confront you with alternative points of view on complex and sensitive issues.

Perhaps the best way to inform yourself is to analyze the positions of those who are regarded as experts and well studied on the issues. It is important to consider every variety of opinion in an attempt to determine the truth. Opinions from the mainstream of society should be examined. Also important are opinions that are considered radical, reactionary, minority or stigmatized by some other uncomplimentary label. An important lesson of history is the fact that many unpopular and even despised opinions eventually gained widespread acceptance. The opinions of Socrates, Jesus and Galileo are good examples of this.

You will approach this book with opinions of your own on the issues debated within it. To have a good grasp of your own viewpoint you must understand the arguments of those with whom you disagree. It is said that those who do not completely understand their adversary's point of view do not fully understand their own.

Perhaps the most persuasive case for considering opposing viewpoints has been presented by John Stuart Mill in his work *On Liberty*. Consider the following statements of his when studying controversial issues.

THE OPINIONS OF OTHERS

If all mankind minus one were of one opinion, and only one person were of the contrary opinion, mankind would be no more justified in silencing that one person than he, if he had the power, would be justified in silencing mankind....

We can never be sure that the opinion we are endeavoring to stifle is a false opinion...

All silencing of discussion is an assumption of infallibility....

Ages are no more infallible than individuals; every age having held many opinions which subsequent ages have deemed not only false but absurd; and it is as certain that many opinions now general will be rejected by future ages....

The only way in which a human being can make some approach to knowing the whole of a subject, is by hearing what can be said about it by persons of every variety of opinion, and studying all modes in which it can be looked at by every character of mind. No wise man ever acquired his wisdom in any mode but this....

The beliefs which we have most warrant for have no safeguard to rest on but a standing invitation to the whole world to prove them unfounded....

To call any proposition certain, while there is any one who would deny its certainty if permitted, but who is not permitted, is to assume that we ourselves and those who agree with us are the judges of certainty, and judges without hearing the other side....

Men are not more zealous for truth than they are for error, and a sufficient application of legal or even social penalties will generally succeed in stopping the propagation of either....

However unwilling a person who has a strong opinion may admit the possibility that his opinion may be false, he ought to be moved by the consideration that, however true it may be, if it is not fully, frequently, and fearlessly discussed, it will be a dead dogma, not a living truth.

I would like to point out to younger readers that John Stuart Mill lived in an era that was not sensitive to terms many people today consider sexist. The words *man* and *mankind* were often used in his work as synonyms for *people* and *humankind.*

A pitfall to avoid in considering alternative points of view is that of regarding your own point of view as being merely common sense and the most rational stance, and the point of view of others as being only opinion and naturally wrong. It may be that the opinion of others is correct and that yours is in error.

Another pitfall to avoid is that of closing your mind to the opinions of those whose views differ from yours. The best way to approach a dialogue is to make your primary purpose that of understanding the mind and arguments of the other person and not that of enlightening him or her with your solutions. One learns more by listening than by speaking.

It is my hope that after reading this book you will have a deeper understanding of the issues debated and will appreciate the complexity of even seemingly simple issues when good and honest people disagree. This awareness is particularly important in a democratic society such as ours, where people enter into public debate to determine the common good. People with whom you disagree should not be regarded as enemies, but rather as friends who suggest a different path to a common goal.

ANALYZING SOURCES OF INFORMATION

The Opposing Viewpoints Series uses diverse sources; magazines, journals, books, newspapers, statements and position papers from a wide range of individuals and organizations. These sources help in the development of a mindset that is open to the consideration of a variety of opinions.

The format of the Opposing Viewpoints Series should help you answer the following questions.

1. *Are you aware that three of the most popular weekly news magazines, Time, Newsweek*, **and** *U.S. News and World Report* **are not totally objective accounts of the news?**
2. **Do you know there is no such thing as a completely objective author, book, newspaper or magazine?**
3. **Do you think that because a magazine or newspaper article is unsigned it is always a statement of facts rather than opinions?**
4. **How can you determine the point of view of newspapers and magazines?**
5. **When you read do you question an author's frame of reference (political persuasion, training, and life experience)?**

Many people finish their formal education unable to cope with these basic questions. They have little chance to understand the social forces and issues surrounding them. Some fall easy victims to demagogues preaching solutions to problems by scapegoating minorities with conspiratorial and paranoid explanations of complex social issues.

I do not want to imply that anything is wrong with authors and publications that have a political slant or bias. All authors have a frame of reference. Readers should understand this. You should also understand that almost all writers have a point of view. An important skill in reading is to be able to locate and identify a point of view. This series gives you practice in both.

DEVELOPING BASIC THINKING SKILLS

A number of basic skills for critical thinking are practiced in the discussion activities that appear throughout the books in the series. Some of the skills are:

Locating a Point of View The ability to determine which side of an issue an author supports.

Evaluating Sources of Information The ability to choose from among alternative sources the most reliable and accurate source in relation to a given subject.

Distinguishing Between Primary and Secondary Sources The ability to understand the important distinction between sources which are primary (original or eyewitness accounts) and those which are secondary (historically removed from, and based on, primary sources).

Separating Fact from Opinion The ability to make the basic distinction between factual statements (those which can be demonstrated or verified empirically) and statements of opinion (those which are beliefs or attitudes that cannot be proved).

Distinguishing Between Prejudice and Reason The ability to differentiate between statements of prejudice (unfavorable, preconceived judgments based on feelings instead of reason) and statements of reason (conclusions that can be clearly and logically explained or justified).

Identifying Stereotypes The ability to identify oversimplified, exaggerated descriptions (favorable or unfavorable) about people and insulting statements about racial, religious or national groups, based upon misinformation or lack of information.

Recognizing Ethnocentrism The ability to recognize attitudes or opinions that express the view that one's own race, culture, or group is inherently superior, or those attitudes that judge another race, culture, or group in terms of one's own.

It is important to consider opposing viewpoints. It is equally important to be able to critically analyze those viewpoints. The discussion activities in this book will give you practice in mastering these thinking skills.

Using this book, and others in the series, will help you develop critical thinking skills. These skills should improve your ability to better understand what you read. You should be better able to separate fact from opinion, reason from rhetoric. You should become a better consumer of information in our media-centered culture.

A VALUES ORIENTATION

Throughout the Opposing Viewpoints Series you are presented conflicting values. A good example is *American Foreign Policy*. The first chapter debates whether foreign policy should be based on the same kind of moral principles that individuals use in guiding their personal actions, or instead be based primarily on doing what best advances national interests, regardless of moral implications.

The series does not advocate a particular set of values. Quite the contrary! The very nature of the series leaves it to you, the reader, to formulate the values orientation that you find most suitable. My purpose, as editor of the series, is to see that this is made possible by offering a wide range of viewpoints which are fairly presented.

David L. Bender
Opposing Viewpoints Series Editor

THE POLITICAL ANIMAL

"Man is a political creature and one whose nature is to live with others"
Aristotle, *Ethics.*

History would seem to support Aristotle's famous contention that people are social and political animals. With extremely rare exceptions, humankind has been (and still is) known to gather in communities of varying sizes. Even the researches of archaeologists indicate that our prehistoric ancestors lived and hunted in bands. It is apparent that the group is able to offer that which the solitary life cannot – security, protection, mutual aid and simple companionship.

Yet it is equally apparent that group life has its negative side. If people must live together in social–political units, they must also reach agreement upon how those units are to be governed. And for all who have lived through political campaigns, witnessed ideological revolutions or fought in civil wars, it should be obvious that agreement is not easily achieved. Indeed, if people could agree universally upon what is the nature and role of government, then political parties, elections, revolutions and the like probably would not be a part of political life.

It is out of this diversity of opinion that the political spectrum rises. The spectrum is essentially a patchwork of ideas relating to crucial political questions. What form of government is best? Within that form of government, what should be the relationship of the government to the governed? Who should hold ultimate power? How should that power be exercised? An individual's position on the spectrum will depend upon his or her answers to these and similar questions.

The purpose of this book is to outline the contemporary political spectrum in American life. Chapter one, **What Is the Political Spectrum?**, attempts to demonstrate two significant facts about the spectrum. First, that disagreement often arises regarding positioning on the spectrum. In other words, opinions frequently will differ over definitions of conservatism, liberalism and extremism. Second, that the spectrum will change with time and circumstance. What is considered liberal today, may be thought of as conservative tomorrow.

Chapters two and three deal with liberalism and conservatism. Supporters and opponents of both principles debate the philosophical and practical value of these "isms." The Irving Kristol viewpoint, in chapter three, should prove of special interest to the reader as it illustrates the changing nature of the spectrum. Kristol, long considered a liberal, has recently found himself labeled a "neo–conservative" (new conservative). As he implies in his viewpoint, neo–conservatives have not necessarily, through the years, changed their opinions on key foreign and domestic issues. Rather, it is the spectrum itself which has changed or "shifted" with time.

Finally, the most elusive part of the spectrum, extremism, is presented in chapter four. It is difficult indeed to reach a consensus upon what extremism is. The editors have attempted to clarify the issue in an essay entitled *"What Extremism Is."* We do not presume that this viewpoint is or should be the final word on the subject. However, it will provide the reader with some basis for evaluating the remaining viewpoints in the chapter.

This anthology of opposing viewpoints on the political spectrum will probably raise more questions than it provides answers. The nature of the spectrum is such that ready answers simply are not available. But that should neither deter nor discourage the reader. Rather, he or she should be mindful of what the acclaimed French writer, Joseph Joubert (1754–1824), once wrote: "It is better to debate a question without settling it than to settle a question without debating it."

Chapter **1**

THE POLITICAL SPECTRUM

What is the Political Spectrum?

"One way to distinguish between liberals and conservatives is by their readiness to accept or bring about change."

The Spectrum as a Straight Line

David L. Bender

The following viewpoint is taken from an earlier work by David L. Bender which appeared in the OPPOSING VIEWPOINTS SERIES. In that anthology, Mr. Bender depicts the spectrum as a "straightline" and relates it to a series of viewpoints on the welfare state. It would prove interesting to compare his conception of the spectrum to the "diamond" in the following viewpoint.

Consider the following questions while reading:

1. **According to Bender, how do liberals differ from conservatives?**
2. **What analogy does Rexford Tugwell use to illustrate the difference between liberals and radicals? Is it a good analogy?**

David L. Bender, *Liberals and Conservatives: A Debate on the Welfare State.* St. Paul: Greenhaven Press, 1973.

The terms, liberal, conservative, radical, extremist and a few similar labels, are perhaps used more than any others in social studies classes, in political conversations and by the communications media. However, it is doubtful that many people have a clear understanding of these terms and the differences they signify. It is difficult to pick up the editorial page of any newspaper without reading about the in-fighting of the liberals and conservatives in either the House or the Senate. One is also likely to read about radical or reactionary groups or interests at work somewhere in our society. Because these terms are so often and so carelessly used, it is important that the interested student and the concerned citizen be able to define them and recognize when they are properly used...

One way to distinguish between liberals and conservatives is by their readiness to accept or bring about change.

READINESS TO CHANGE

If one were to construct a continuum showing the reaction to change, the following stopping points would be noted:

THE POLITICAL SPECTRUM

Radicals   Liberals   Conservatives   Reactionaries

Left Wing   Right Wing

Radicals and liberals are called left-wingers or leftists and welcome change. Conservatives and reactionaries are called right-wingers or rightists and are quite reluctant to accept change. If each position on the continuum were defined it would read as follows:

The Radical   He favors a radical or basic change. He is quite impatient and would quickly support a revolution to bring about the desired change.

The Liberal   He is ready to move forward and accept change but would be considered a reformer rather than a revolutionary.

19

The Conservative   He is quite content with things the way they are.

The Reactionary   He wants change also, but wants to retreat into the past and restore the order of things the way they used to be.

TRAIN STATION ANALOGY

A former advisor of Franklin D. Roosevelt's, Rexford Tugwell, skillfully uses the example of a community's need for a new train station to illustrate the difference between liberals and radicals: *"Liberals would like to rebuild the station while the trains are running; radicals prefer to blow up the station and forego service until the new structure is built."*[1] One might add that conservatives would prefer to keep the old station, being satisfied with it, while reactionaries would abandon the station entirely since they do not approve of trains in the first place.*

Whatever the differences between the left-wing and the right-wing in accepting change, all four viewpoints are helpful to society. The radical points out the future's possibilities while the liberal helps to see them realized through the practice of compromise. The conservative cautions us to preserve past accomplishments and the reactionary reminds us of our heritage and the glory of times past.

1. Rexford G. Tugwell, *The Industrial Discipline and the Governmental Arts* (New York: Columbia University Press, 1934-5), p. 229.
* In this hypothetical situation, the reader must consider the need for a new train station and the method of building it open to question, otherwise the liberal solution would appear to be the only prudent one.

"Thus, we can define 'rightist' political philosophies as those favoring economic liberties...and 'leftist' philosophies as those favoring civil liberties..."

The Spectrum as a Diamond

Ferdinand V. Solara

In an effort to present a visual outline of the political spectrum, many authors have resorted to geometric designs, the circle being one of the most popular. In his book, *Key Influences in the American Right*, Ferdinand V. Solara maintains that "the spectrum of possible political philosophies can adequately be represented by using a diagram resembling a baseball diamond."

Consider the following questions while reading:
1. **What are the differences between the highest and lowest points of the diamond?**
2. **According to Solara, how do liberals differ from conservatives?**

I believe the spectrum of possible political philosophies can adequately be represented by using a diagram resembling a baseball diamond:

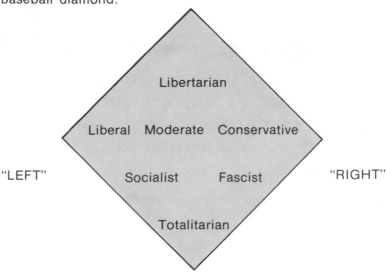

THE THREE BASES

On this diagram, the uppermost point ("second base") represents the theoretical condition of absolute liberty, while the bottom point ("home plate") represents its antithesis, absolute slavery. As one progresses upward on the diagram, one encounters political systems offering ever–increasing amounts of individual liberty; conversely, as one moves downward, the opposite holds true.

Moving *across* the diagram horizontally, at any given level (from left to right), one encounters systems where the *total amount* of individual liberty is equivalent, but the *nature of the restrictions* on liberty is different. The further to the *left* you go (towards "third base"), you will find an increasingly greater relative proportion of civil (or social) liberty, and an increasingly smaller proportion of economic liberty. As you move to the *right* (towards "first base"), the opposite is true.

Thus, we can define "rightist" political philosophies as those favoring economic liberties, to at least some degree, over civil liberties, and "leftist" philosophies as those favoring civil liberties over economic liberties.

"A conservative accepts man's inequalities as part of his heritage and considers liberty and property to have priority over equality."

A Conservative Views the Spectrum

George A. Reimann

George A. Reimann is the current Vice President of the Tennessee State Rifle Association. A conservative writer, Reimann believes that the key to understanding the ideas of liberalism and conservatism lies in an historical analysis of the terms. The following viewpoint, originally entitled *A Rational Explanation*, attempts such an analysis.

Consider the following questions while reading:
1. **According to Reimann, how do liberals differ from conservatives?**
2. **How did Rousseau, Marx and Burke contribute to the concepts of liberalism and conservatism?**

George A. Reimann, "A Rational Explanation." Reprinted from *Life Lines*, Vol. 14, No. 24, February 25, 1972.

When the terms "Liberalism" and "Conservatism" are bandied about, it is evident that few Americans fully comprehend the concepts associated with these terms. The dictionary yields: Liberalism — favorable to progress or reform, as in political or religious reform; noting or pertaining to a political party advocating measures of progressive political reform; Conservatism — noting or pertaining to a political party whose characteristic principle is opposition to change in the institutions of a country. Boiled down to the residue, Liberalism equals innovation and Conservatism equals opposition. Satisfied?

An encyclopedia may be more enlightening, but here the emphasis is not on any uniqueness of American Liberalism and Conservatism, but on their histories. And as the evolution of these philosophies is traced, the trail grows colder as it nears the present time. A lingering impression persists of innovation vs. opposition, or good guys against bad guys.

LIBERAL ORIGINS

Now it's our turn, and if you have already wagered that liberals will come in second, you can collect now. The term "liberal" stems from the word "liberalis" — pertaining to a free man. "Free man" in the context of current American Liberalism is largely based upon the philosophical theories of Jean-Jacques Rousseau (1712-1778). Rousseau did not invent Liberalism, however, he was an author and political theorist of considerable intellect and his philosophical forays included advocacy of popular sovereignty and a theory of democratic government. But having given credit where it was due, it must be observed that Rousseau became increasingly alienated from the established social and political order of his time. His "Discourse on the Origin and Bases of Inequality Among Men" (1754) indicted the political state and the concept of private property while it glorified "natural man." As Rousseau saw it, "natural man" was inherently good and feelings and emotions were the "primary values" in life. But natural man's primary values were corrupted by his own relationships, his institutions, and his environment. Civilization itself was to blame for man's impressive inventory of vices...

One is reluctant to invite Karl Marx into a critique of Liberalism, for to do so is to cause hysterical howls of indignant protest which drown out all subsequent discussion. Yet Karl Marx must enter, even if uninvited. Marx was one of many convinced of man's inherent goodness, believing that when the victims of capitalism, the working class, overthrew the owning class by violent revolution, wisdom and justice would miraculously accrue to the workers, thereby enabling them to rule the world beneficently. Marx concluded: "Qualities of human intelligence, personality, emotional and religious life merely reflect man's economic environment. The evil man does is just a reflection of his environment." Thus, if man's environment were corrected, his nature would automatically transform so that he would work according to his ability and desire to receive only according to his needs.

MARX AND SHAW

The Fabian Socialists organized in 1884, a year after Marx's death. The Fabians planned to reorganize society by gradually transferring control of property and capital from individuals to the "community" for the "general benefit," thereby establishing a socialistic, one-world order. George Bernard Shaw, a Fabian founder and its most articulate spokesman, endorsed Marx's Utopian concept of compulsory equality of condition but deplored open class warfare and violent revolution...

LIBERAL MYTHS

I suppose I am still a liberal within the original meaning of that much abused word, although having learned through experience more than is dreamed of in the philosophy of most Western liberals, I no longer share their faith in the inevitability of progress and the perfectibility of man through the creation of a better material environment.

Freda Utley in her *Odyssey of a Liberal*

So the Fabians began working for change by indoctrinating the young scholars. Eventually, they believed, these "intellectual' revolutionaries would acquire great power and influence in the opinion making and power wielding agencies of the world. In practice it meant slow, piecemeal changes in established concepts of morality, law, government, economics, and education. The Fabians rejected all suggestions that they form their own party, preferring to impose their influence and to change everything by administrative infiltration of existing educational institutions, political parties, civil service, etc. Salvation by subterfuge!...

Liberalism is said to have matured in America during the social and economic changes wrought by the industrial revolution in the 19th century. Free enterprise and self reliance were in high esteem. Relative to earlier times, a high degree of individual liberty and freedom of action were achieved. But things were far from perfect. Inequalities and injustice were still evident everywhere in various forms. Liberals of that time brought pressure to bear on government to restrict individual freedom where it appeared to cause inequality. But inequalities persisted. Answer: More coercive government control...

CONSERVATIVE ORIGINS

Were the definition of Conservatism restricted to its being the opposite (or opposition) of Liberalism, then the preceding text might pass as a definition, with apologies for indicating what something is by describing what it is not. But such a restriction assumes the pre-existence of Liberalism in order that Conservatism may rise to oppose it when in fact Conservatism signifies the established order which Liberalism seeks to change.

Scholars credit Edmund Burke (1729-1797) with laying the foundation for modern Conservative thought. Burke's philosophy does not lend itself readily to a summary, and a condensation risks injustice. Burke held to Christian theology and morality in expressing a coherent view of social order based on natural law. He believed that to achieve liberty and justice, a government must be in harmony with historical experience; that an enduring government is a contract of the eternal society, a willing obligation to the dead, the living, and those yet unborn. A viable government is not an artificial contrivance of the intellectual whims of the moment. Individuals are foolish but the species is wise, and the wisdom of the species, the natural aristocracy, should govern, preserving the method of nature in the conduct of the state, while blending the best of the old order into the changes required for society's survival.

Conservatism extends beyond Burke's views of the proper relationship between the government and the governed. Conservative tenets recognize that men are unequal in terms of ambition, ability, intelligence, and character; that human reason is prone to error, of limited reach, and often governed by emotion; that liberty takes precedence over equality, so that one cannot infringe upon the liberty of another in the name of equality; and that one must be free to choose between right and wrong and accept responsibility for the consequences of his actions...

WALK OR RUN

I believe, that liberals tend to design houses, conservatives to build them. The liberal mind, by and large, moves more quickly than the conservative's to original thought.

Those of us on the right tend to stand by tradition, precedent, and the old ways of doing things; those on the left are more impatient to get on with the job.

James J. Kilpatrick, *Washington Star*, May, 1973.

LIBERTY VS EQUALITY

To summarize, a Liberal strives to achieve equality among men and believes that inequalities result from factors in man's environment. Various "unfavorable" experiences during a lifetime cause a person to misbehave. If a suitable environment were devised (presumably by the government), man would cease being such a difficult creature and would become instead equal and agreeable. A Conservative accepts man's inequalities as part of his heritage and considers liberty and property to have priority over equality. Man must be free to make his own choices, not intrude into the affairs of others, and be responsible for his actions. Government should be guided by the sure footing of proven philosophies, and minimize its control over one's private affairs by functioning only to maintain the order and justice required to perpetuate a well-organized society.

"It is time to end the futile quarrel between 'liberals' and conservatives... we are all liberals, we are all conservatives."

A Liberal Views the Spectrum

Henry Steele Commager

Henry Steele Commager is one of America's leading liberal historians. He has authored numerous books (*The American Mind, The Empire of Reason,* and others) and scholarly articles and regularly contributes editorials to leading newspapers throughout the country. In the following viewpoint, he shows why political labeling can be misleading.

Consider the following questions while reading:

1. **List Commager's seven distinguishing features of liberalism.**
2. **What did Alexander Hamilton feel the role of government should be?**
3. **According to Commager, how do liberals differ from conservatives?**

Henry Steele Commager, "Liberalism, Conservatism Are Two Sides of the Same American Coin," *Los Angeles Times,* December 3, 1979. Reprinted with permission of the author.

Recently the National Conservative Political Action Committee placed a full page advertisement critical of Sen. Edward M. Kennedy, D-Mass., in newspapers throughout the United States. It asked the following question of the American people: "What makes you think that an extreme liberal is able to make a good president?" It is astonishing that the term liberal is now a dirty word.

ORIGINS OF THE WORD

What is meant by liberalism?

The word "liberal" comes from the same root-word as does the word "liberty" — the Latin *liber*, which means "free." Its repudiation by modern conservatives constitutes a failure to understand the historical roots of conservatism as well as a failure to understand the nature of liberalism.

Those who use the terms liberal and liberalism in a pejorative sense would do well to consult dictionaries, American and English alike, for enlightenment. All give the same definitions: a liberal is one who is "free from prejudice," who "supports religious freedom and the right to dissent;" who is "favorable to changes and reforms leading in the direction of freedom or democracy;" who is "tolerant of the ideas of others;" or who is "generous and open-hearted." In the headlong retreat from liberalism are we now to commit ourselves to intolerance, prejudice and conformity? Historically, the "liberal arts" are those worthy of "free men;" are we to turn now to those studies that are not fit for free men?

As those and a score of other definitions make clear, liberalism is not a particular program but rather a philosophical attitude.

FEATURES OF LIBERALISM

What are the distinguishing features of that liberalism that have now become so fashionable to regard with suspicion?

First, a passion for what Thomas Jefferson called the "illimitable freedom of the human mind" and an "uncompromising hostility to every form of tyranny over the minds of men," whether that be political, religious or military.

Second, a repudiation of the tyranny of ignorance, of poverty and of vice, because these deny or inhibit the exercise of true freedom.

Third, a faith in reason and in the ability of men to govern themselves when their minds are liberated by education and their judgments protected by the orderly processes of the law.

Fourth, respect for the dignity of every individual — a respect that requires equal rights and equal justice in law and society.

Fifth, an acceptance of the will of the majority as long as that will operates under the law, with respect for the rights and interests of minorities.

Sixth, a commitment to the principle that the earth belongs to the living, not the dead, and that while we have an obligation to preserve what is best in the past, our primary fiduciary obligation is to posterity.

Seventh, the Jeffersonian belief — a belief that animated the generation of the Founding Fathers — that people have an inalienable right to pursue and obtain happiness.

REAL CONSERVATIVES?

Increasing numbers of Americans evidently regard themselves as conservatives, even though they have only a foggy notion of what the term implies. They seem simply to like the sound of the word.

James J. Kilpatrick, *Washington Star,* February, 1978.

It will not escape those familiar with American history that much of this agenda is also the agenda of conservatism. In the United States, liberalism and conservatism have been, from the beginning, two sides of the same coin, and our greatest liberals — Thomas Jefferson, Abraham Lincoln and Franklin D. Roosevelt — also have been our greatest conservatives.

GOVERNMENT AS UMPIRE

Conservatism, as defined by its philosophical father Edmund Burke, rested on three foundations: the monarchy, the church and tradition. Liberalism, as explained by John Stuart Mill and Herbert Spencer, meant that government should keep its hands off the social and economic activities of its citizens and content itself with keeping order and enforcing the law. As Spencer put it, government should be "anarchy plus the policeman."

Though many of our modern conservatives still accept Burke's philosophy, they also accept the liberal concept of government as umpire. Neither view has anything whatever to do with the American experience. Because America had no monarchy, no church and little tradition, its citizens could give a different and more sensible meaning to conservatism. In America, conservatism has sought to conserve the natural resources of soil, water, forests and air; to conserve, and prosper, the dignity of every individual man and woman so that they could enjoy to the fullest that liberty and equality which Nature and God had bestowed upon them, and to conserve that heritage of arts, science, religion and law that we call civilization...

LOOK TO THE PAST

It would not be necessary to remind even the most purblind conservatives of all if they knew their own history — which they do not. They inextricably link the history of conservatism

Henry Steele Commager

31

with that of the Republican Party, forgetting that the Grand Old Party has often tried to be a government of the people. Most conservatives have forgotten that Alexander Hamilton, the spiritual father of both conservatism and the Republican Party, was the most ardent champion of a strong central government in our entire history; and they have forgotten that it was Hamilton who asserted that "all the underground wealth" belonged, as a matter of course, to the national government "to be disposed of by Congress as it saw fit for the best interests of the nation." They have forgotten, too, that it was the first Republican Party that *liberated* the slaves, and wrote into the Constitution the 14th Amendment that quite effectively legally legitimized governmental centralization.

They choose not to remember that in the golden age of conservative politics — the age of Theodore Roosevelt, Elihu Root, Albert Beveridge and William Howard Taft — it was the Republican Party that maintained a government powerful enough to intervene aggressively in the domestic economy and in world affairs. By insisting on a hard and fast division between conservatives and liberals, between Republicans and Democrats, many of today's conservatives ignore the fact that since President Woodrow Wilson's administration the two parties have wrestled themselves into each other's clothes...

In his first inaugural address, given in 1801, Thomas Jefferson said, "We are all republicans." We should heed his words. It is time to end the futile quarrel between "liberals" (who often demonstrate as little awareness of their own history as do "conservatives"), and conservatives. If our society is to recover the unity that it must have to survive, it must recognize that we are all Democrats, we are all Republicans, we are all federalists, we are all nationalists, we are all liberals, we are all conservatives.

"Many Americans who now call themselves conservatives would be liberals under the older meaning of the word."

The Spectrum Keeps Changing

Joseph C. Harsch

Joseph C. Harsch is a columnist for the *Christian Science Monitor* whose column appears thrice weekly in the Monitor's Opinion and Commentary page. He joined the Monitor in 1929 and has served in various capacities including war correspondent during World War II. In the following viewpoint on liberalism vs. conservatism, Harsch offers some incisive comments on political labeling and mislabeling.

Consider the following questions while reading:

1. **According to Harsch, how do liberals differ from conservatives?**
2. **What was the original meaning of liberalism?**
3. **Why would today's conservatives be considered yesterday's liberals?**

Liberal vs. conservative — what really is meant by those two words?

An old and respected friend of mine thinks he knows the difference. He calls himself a conservative. He goes white in the face and splutters when he has to use the hated word "liberal." His intensity is such that you would almost think he was a Roman Catholic speaking of Protestants, or vice versa, back in the days of the religious wars when they joyfully burned each other at the stake, singing hymns the while. But when asked to identify what he means by "liberal" he only says, "someone who enjoys spending other people's money."

DISTORTED USAGE

What do people who think of themselves as "liberals" mean when they spit out the word "conservative" with equal intensity? They mean someone totally selfish who cares nothing for the community as a whole, but solely about what he can take from the system.

What a pity that two fine words, liberal and conservative, have been so debased and distorted in American political usage. Conservative once meant a person concerned about preserving the best in the social and political heritage. It did not mean and certainly should not mean a layer of rich and powerful who use public office largely for their own selfish, personal or class profit. Edmund Burke thought he was being conservative when he spoke out in Parliament against measures intended to coerce the fractious American colonists. Benjamin Disraeli thought he was being conservative when he introduced legislation to reduce and eventually prohibit such monstrous things as children being used to pull carts in coal mines.

CHANGING MEANINGS

Liberal once meant to favor a free, marketplace economy. It meant freedom from government intrusion into and management of the marketplace. It meant the right of the industrious merchant or manufacturer to invest his money as he chose. It meant the opposite of everything that happens in either a fascist or a communist society.

Many Americans who now call themselves conservatives would be liberals under the older meaning of the word. Most American liberals are conservative in the sense that they care

34

about the welfare and the happiness of the American people, who are, after all, the country's most valuable asset. To try to conserve their health and increase their productivity is properly speaking, a conservative thing to do.

The meaning of these words has changed radically in very recent times. For example, in current American usage conservative tends to mean someone who would double American military spending and avoid any accommodation with the Soviet Union. Yet only some 25 years ago conservatives opposed high military spending and American intervention against communist regimes overseas.

WOLF OR LAMB?

The conservative errs in regarding man as though he were a wolf; the liberal errs in regarding man as though he were a lamb; neither will concede that man is both in nearly equal portion.

Sydney Harris, Field Enterprises, April, 1980.

Pre-World War II American conservatives were isolationist.

And, oddly enough as it seems now, early New Deal "liberals" preached "America first," in the sense of economic isolationism and regarded Herbert Hoover as a dangerous "internationalist."

UNDERSTANDING STEREOTYPES

A stereotype is an oversimplified or exaggerated description of people or things. Stereotyping can be favorable. However, most stereotyping tends to be highly uncomplimentary and, at times, degrading.

Stereotyping grows out of our prejudices. When we stereotype someone, we are prejudging him or her. Consider the following example: Mr. X is convinced that all Mexicans are lazy, sloppy and careless people. The Diaz family, a family of Mexicans, happen to be his next-door neighbors. One evening, upon returning home from work, Mr. X notices that the garage pails in the Diaz driveway are overturned and that the rubbish is scattered throughout the driveway. He immediately says to himself: "Isn't that just like those lazy, sloppy and careless Mexicans?" The possibility that a group of neighborhood vandals or a pack of stray dogs may be responsible for the mess never enters his mind. Why not? Simply because he has prejudged all Mexicans and will keep his stereotype consistent with his prejudice. The famous (or infamous) Archie Bunker of television fame is a classic example of our Mr. X.

(At age 14) "They ought to do more for pensioners."

(Age 24) "Pensioners? Yes, but can we afford it?"

(Age 34) "I agree, but higher pensions means higher taxes."

(Age 44) "More for pensioners? Certainly, but what would it cost?"

(Age 54) "We'd all like pensions to be raised, but . . ."

(Age 64) "They ought to do more for pensioners."

PART I

The illustration above represents what may be called the "evolution of a stereotype." It depicts the attitudes toward pensioners held by individuals at various ages in their life.

Instructions

STEP 1

Each individual should analyze the illustration and answer the following: Do you feel that the illustration does fall into the category of stereotyping? (That is, is the illustration based upon fact or upon prejudgement of the six age groups depicted?)

STEP 2

The class should break into groups of four to six students. The students within each group should discuss and defend their answers.

PART II

STEP 1

The following class project would be useful in testing your answers and conclusions. Each member of the class should interview individuals within the six age groups. The people interviewed should be asked about their attitude toward pensioners and why they hold that opinion. The interviews may be conducted among family members, church groups etc. and at public places such as shopping centers.

STEP 2

The results of the interviews should be tallied and discussed at a general class meeting.

PART III

Read through the following list carefully. Mark *S* for any statement that is an example of stereotyping. Mark *N* for any statement that is not an example of stereotyping. Mark *U* if you are undecided about any statement. Then discuss and compare your decisions with other class members.

S = Stereotype
N = Not a stereotype
U = Undecided

_____ 1. Political conservatives are opposed to the social security system.

_____ 2. Liberals, as a group, tend to be more sympathetic to the needs and desires of the poor and minorities.

_____ 3. An individual who calls himself a staunch economic conservative would be opposed to government interference in the affairs of big business.

_____ 4. Conservatives dress and act more conservatively than liberals.

_____ 5. Members of the Communist Party of the United States favor the overthrow of the present system of government.

_____ 6. College students tend to hold very liberal social, economic and political views.

_____ 7. Members of the American Nazi Party and the Ku Klux Klan are racists.

_____ 8. All blacks in America favor the welfare system.

_____ 9. All whites in America are opposed to the welfare system.

_____ 10. Some women support the ERA.

_____ 11. A "macho" male type would be opposed to woman's liberation.

_____ 12. Extreme liberal thinkers are communist sympathizers.

Chapter **2**

THE POLITICAL SPECTRUM

What is Liberalism?

"Men could never knowingly choose not to be free, in the liberal view, without ceasing to be human."

What Liberalism Is

David Sidorsky

A professor of philosophy at Columbia University, David Sidorsky has written extensively in the areas of social and political theory. In the following reading, he views liberalism as a "secular faith" and examines its conception of the nature of man, society and history.

Consider the following questions while reading:

1. According to the author, what are the three tenets of liberalism?
2. How does a liberal view the history of humankind?

David Sidorsky, *The Liberal Tradition in European Thought.* New York: G.P. Putnam's Sons, 1971. Copyright © 1970 by Educational Resources Corporation. Reprinted with permission of the publisher.

When liberalism is considered as a secular faith, its central vision is a conception of the nature of man, of society, and of history. In simplest terms, it is, **first**, a conception of man as desiring freedom and capable of exercising rational free choice. **Second**, it is a perspective on social institutions as open to rational reconstruction in the light of individual needs. It is, **third**, a view of history as progressively perfectible through the continuous application of human reason to social institutions.

1. FREEDOM AND MAN

Although it is not possible to logically deduce any of the specific programs of liberalism from its conception of human nature, these programs would seem to presuppose that man is capable of freedom. For unless he were, there would seem to be no point to the whole range of liberal effort, from acts of toleration in the seventeenth century to the extension of suffrage to women in the twentieth, which defend a person's right to exercise his freedom or extend the areas in which it can be exercised. Unless men wanted freedom and could make reasonable use of it, there would seem to be no passionate preference for the elimination of censorship or of prescribed belief or even of many forms of coercion...

Critics of liberalism have suggested that men fear freedom and are anxious to escape it through the acceptance of tradition or authority, but have found their empirical evidence discounted. Men reject freedom, the liberals reply, because they are sick or coerced or ignorant or desperate or believe that they are attaining a greater measure of freedom. Men could never knowingly choose not to be free, in the liberal view, without ceasing to be human.

2. FREEDOM AND REASON

Secondly, for men to exercise the degree of rational free choice which liberalism envisages, the major institutions of society must admit of reform and revision...

Man's position in the social order, that is, his status, power, vocation, and wealth, in the traditional view before the period of modern liberalism, were considered to be, in great measure, the product of birth and custom. In liberal theory, the doctrine of rationality of men is developed to suggest that all men are equal, hence, the stress upon equal opportunity with careers open to talents without antecedent determination of political or social position. Any fixed social or economic order could be

42

restructured in the light of individual effort or by the aggregating of individual preferences.

This liberal attitude to church, state, and social hierarchy of course reflected the transformation of these institutions in Western Europe in a period of the rise of science, secularism, and capitalism. Liberalism was both the product and, in part, the shaper of that transformation...

LIBERALISM AND FREEDOM

This, perhaps, is the testament of Liberalism. For underlying all the specific projects which men espouse who think of themselves as Liberals there is always, it seems to me, a deeper concern. It is fixed upon the importance of remaining free in mind and action before changing circumstances.

This is why Liberalism has always been associated with a passionate interest in freedom of thought and freedom of speech, in scientific research, in experiment, in the liberty of teaching, In an independent and unbiased press, in the right of men to differ in their opinions and to be different in their conduct...

Walter Lippmann

---

3. UNDERSTANDING HISTORY

The third aspect of liberalism as secular faith is its approach to understanding human history. The interpretation of the past provides the frame of reference for its political and social programs. For liberalism, history is the arena of human progress and perfectibility. In the background of many of the specific programs or theses of liberalism there is implicit the doctrine that the correct and repeated application of human reason to any social evil — war, poverty, illness, prejudice, or any of the terrors of the apocalypse or primal curses of the human estate — can mitigate their ravages and gradually but effectively eliminate each and all of them without any foreseeable limit to the process. If human history is full of atrocity and evil, it is because man has not yet educated himself to overcome the ignorance imposed by corrupt institutions.

43

"The fact that the American liberal is, and sees himself as, the guardian of the traditional values of the country, cannot be overestimated."

America is Better for Liberalism

Henry Fairlie

Many liberals have long contended that it is the liberal who supports and defends the history and traditional values of America. In the following viewpoint, Henry Fairlie, a liberal editorialist, strengthens this contention by depicting the lives of Ruth and David, a hypothetical liberal couple.

Consider the following questions while reading:
1. **What does Fairlie understand to be the "geological fault" of liberals?**
2. **According to Fairlie, who are the more traditional: American liberals or conservatives?**
3. **Do you believe that liberalism, as defined by Fairlie, will be dead in the eighties? Explain your answer.**

Henry Fairlie, "Is Liberalism Dead?", *The New Republic*, April 17, 1976. Reprinted by permission of THE NEW REPUBLIC, © 1976 The New Republic, Inc.

We are being told on every side that the American liberal is no more; that none of the issues with which he is concerned any longer have much appeal to the public; and that even the liberal candidates this year would prefer not to have the label strung about their necks, but instead be known as progressive...

There is something implausible in these obituary notices. Great political movements — ideas — ideologies, if one wishes to call them that — simply do not die that way. In fact, we need to realize that the great "-isms" of the modern age — not the vile "-isms" like Nazism — have a genuine life. They survive because they represent realities: ways in which people perceive the world today, respond to it and deal with it, and above all try to make it...

THE MODERN FAMILY

We know that our world would not be as decent and restless and caring a place as it manages to be if the American liberal had not been so dominant a figure in it. He and she deserve to be criticized — they will be criticized here — but as I personalize them, Ruth and David, let us remember how we would miss them.

Ruth and David are not childless. On the contrary, they seem to have determined to maintain the reproduction rate of the species, and therefore have not been satisfied with the two-child family. Moreover, since they believe that a family should be a democracy — like the direct democracy of the Greek city states in which every citizen participates — they have had enough children to populate the family with enough citizens. The modern family is usually thought to be a conservative institution, the conservative its true defender. But it is Ruth and David who really maintain the family in a world unfriendly to it...

Ruth and David are intense, not only in their care for their children, but in their celebration of their ancestors. They are the real keepers of photograph albums. They will bridge the generation gap, even if it means manufacturing a generation gap to bridge. It is they who tell how their mothers baked a cake, and their fathers read Emerson to them every night. It is they who want to bake a cake as their mothers baked, and read Emerson aloud to their children as their fathers read. Like the Greek city state itself, the American liberal family is one of the most consciously controlled environments that can be imagined.

45

A BETTER SOCIETY

Liberals embrace a positive, activist role for the State and the Federal Government...and believe we have a special obligation to the weak, the poor and the unorganized. They believe the redistributive effect of social-assistance programs benefits everybody by stimulating the economy and reducing crime and the incidence of physical and mental breakdown.

George McGovern, former senator, South Dakota

And this matters, for at first it can seem repulsive. With every nod to permissiveness, with every inquiry to the infant about whether it wants to be breast-fed—and it *will* be breast-fed, like it or not—and when—and it *will* be every four hours, like it or not—with every vote taken to decide when the children may first enjoy sex, the family is very strongly led and directed—and maintained.

This is one of the problems of the American liberal, of Ruth and David. They will be out on the streets at the drop of a hat, to assert the right of everyone else to "do their own thing," but they themselves are intensely concerned to pass on the values of their parents, and the values of their grandparents. It is they—and not those who are said to be conservative—who know exactly the day on which their grandparents first landed in New York. Ruth and David want to rear other Ruths and Davids, and to pass on values and attitudes that were passed on to them.

I emphasize this point, because I think that it is crucial and unrecognized, and because it points immediately to the strengths and weaknesses of the American liberal. Ruth and David are guardians; in their own lives, they are the pre-servers of values. Yet again and again, in their public concerns, they seem to be tolerant of a social environment which must erode those values...

THE LIBERAL FAULT

This geological fault in the liberal is one of the keys to his present ineffectiveness. Ruth and David wish their own children to be well educated; but they support *for others* every simple-minded "experimental" program that would reduce education to little more than play-therapy. They want their own children to be able to read; but they support *for others* methods of teaching which are based on the assumption that the way to learn to read is not to learn to read, but instead to cut out colored pieces of paper, and so let the child "express" itself. They do not like to see their own children stoned; but they support *for others* a permissiveness that can reduce a child to inertia and fecklessness. They do not care for porno-graphy; but they support *for others* the right to publish any obscenity.

There is a profound elitism in this; let the traditional values of everyone else go to pot—almost literally—but we will maintain the benefits of those traditional values for ourselves and our children. This is the fault: the slippage in the liberal of which ordinary people are aware...

47

TOMORROW'S LIBERALS

Somewhere along the political way, the word "liberal" fell into disrepute. No kindly dictionary definition of the word can save it; none of its past laurels are sufficient to rescue it from the edge of popular disdain. Only the future actions of those who believe in liberalism can restore the word's dignity.

Leigh Lerner, *Minneapolis Star*, January 9, 1980

GUARDIANS OF VALUES

The fact that the American liberal is, and sees himself as, the guardian of the traditional values of the country, cannot be overestimated. Ruth and David are more a part of what America has been made since the mass immigration, of what it has been made in the past century, than any conservative. Since the end of World War I, the Republican party and the Democratic party have occupied the White House for the same number of years: yet the Republicans have not left their stamp on the country in the same way as the Democrats. It is in this profound sense that Ruth and David are the guardians of the values without which this country cannot recognize itself...

AMERICAN LIBERALS

Finally, Ruth and David need to come to terms with the fact that, whereas in Europe it is the conservative who is the guardian of the history and traditions and values of the nation, in America it is the liberal. Ruth and David should this year reoccupy the land they made; and perhaps they should begin by recalling the laughter in the face of Franklin Roosevelt, and recognizing a laughter that may be as warm.

Ruth and David! Your record over the years is proud. You have little for which to apologize. You have suffered many wounds for your country, but you are not scarred. You are not dead; you can afford not to have a loser. Listen to your country, for it wants to listen to you. Put aside your embroidery at least for this year; the tapestry of your country and your tradition is made of more than little stitches. It is made of your own lustfulness for your land and your time; the "glow that goes beyond energy" is made from your decency. Go out and claim your land; the land is waiting to be claimed by you.

48

"I resent the assumption of liberals that only they truly understand human needs and suffering."

America is Worse for Liberalism

Ben Stein

Ben Stein is a former columnist for the *Wall Street Journal* and a former member of Richard Nixon's speech-writing staff. In the following viewpoint, Stein offers a categorical series of personal complaints directed at liberals and liberalism in America.

Consider the following questions while reading:
1. What examples of "liberal hypocrisy" does the author give?
2. Give at least two examples of what Stein considers to be the liberal "double standard."
3. What are the author's attitudes toward welfare?

Ben Stein, "Why Liberals Give Me a Pain in the Neck," *Human Events*, November 27, 1976. Reprinted with permission of *Human Events* magazine.

What I don't like is the way rich liberals, who have made their money through the operations of the capitalist system and who would be miserable bureaucratic cogs in a Socialist system, are nevertheless Socialists. I suspect that a large part of their motivation is a style of asceticism which has been fashionable among the rich since the time of the Pharisees. Another motivation for the rich liberals to dislike the capitalist system is that they have already gotten theirs and they don't want to be challenged by other people coming along and getting theirs.

LIBERALS AND MORALS

I don't like the way liberals of any income group assume that they have a monopoly on morality and that the only conscionable position on issues is their position. A sanctimoniousness runs in the liberal mind which is a direct descendent of the Calvinist assuredness of moral superiority.

Liberals assume that any challenge to their position comes from impure motives, often motivations having to do with "profit and loss" instead of the "human" factors that liberals allegedly consider. I resent the assumption of liberals that only they truly understand human needs and suffering.

I especially resent the claims of white liberals that they know best about how to solve the problems of the poor and the black. There is hardly any evidence that liberal programs to help the poor and the black have done much good. The ordinary operations of the capitalist system, however, have made enormous gains economically for the poor and the black. Liberals don't seem to understand that if they take a dollar from one person and give it to another, there is rarely any benefit. If the economic system produces new dollars for everyone, everyone benefits.

Liberals who send their children to private schools while advocating busing are particularly distasteful. The liberals who plead for integration of someone else's children are particularly blind to their hypocrisy.

CORPORATIONS ARE PEOPLE

I resent the notion that everything that corporations do is wrong and everything that "people" do is right. Liberals don't understand that corporations *are* people. They are the people who work for the corporation, buy its products, and own its stock. There is no mechanical person who is benefited if corporations make a good profit. Real people benefit, just as real people lose when corporations lose money.

I don't like it particularly when liberals say that more money for this or that project can come out of profits. Most people don't realize that profits are small parts of total earnings for most companies and that without the profits, people, even liberals, wouldn't invest their money.

LIBERAL HYPOCRISY

We wanted to save a few bucks to take care of our future. We got inflation. When our kids went to college, the liberal professors either ignored or mocked the values we had taught them at home and in our schools. We've been used, manipulated and scorned—and now liberals want us to come back to the fold.

William F. Gavin, Author, *Street Corner Conservative.*

And there is nothing wrong with big profits. It's a sign of good management and creativity, which are rewarded in the artistic sphere as they should be in the management area. And the stockholders who get the dividends for those profits are often widows and orphans and most of all, pension funds. The liberals' idea that profits all go into buying Balmain gowns is just dangerous nonsense.

PROGRESSIVE EDUCATION

I resent the influence that liberals have gotten over our educational system. Even in those schools which are other than jungles of fear, students don't learn anything. Liberal parents and teachers who have seized control of the schools teach "sensitivity" and "interpersonal relations" to children who barely know how to read and write because the basics have been so badly neglected. Students will have more in life if they know how to read and write than if they have had "peer group effectiveness" training. Children who are without financial resources are not being done any favors if they are not taught how to perform the basic skills with which to earn a living...

I am annoyed at the condescending way liberals look at religion and patriotism. Both of those are forces which make a people work and sacrifice for others and are genuine altru-

51

"Hey, Dad! Why do you call yourself a liberal when you act like a conservative?"

istic forces. Yet liberals scoff at them. Liberals should try to think whether this country could have been built without a sense of mission greater than the love of government money. In fact, liberals ought to think whether or not their own feelings do not constitute a religion of sorts before they make fun of others' religious practices. They might consider whether or not they have a double standard for people who think like they do as compared to people who have different thoughts...

MISPLACED WELFARE

The liberal attitude about welfare is also worth getting furious about. They are tender and sympathetic towards the mother of 10 illegitimate children who is being supported by the taxpayers through Aid to Families with Dependent Children. Who said that that woman should be allowed to make so many mistakes and then have the state make up her losses? The liberal doesn't care about the working poor who might want to have another child but don't because they can't pay for the child. But for the irresponsible people who live off welfare, there is endless sympathy.

That is yet another aspect of the double standard, and there are more. The liberal wants to make a state in which people who have worked hard and abided by the rules are taxed to death to pay for those who do not work at anything except reproducing themselves. The liberal wants a state in which the lower- and middle-middle classes bear the brunt of all social change, while the liberals sit back with their union pay, or university pay, or inherited pay, or money they have gotten from the system they hate, and watch the action.

Another instance of the liberal lack of concern with real compassion is their attitude about environmental issues. No one doubts that there are important environmental problems. But there are also people whose jobs depend on taking a close look at environmental issues and not running off half-cocked whenever a cockroach is threatened. Trees may have rights, but they don't have as many rights as people...

I RESENT, I RESENT

I resent also a kind of cultural imperialism which dominates liberal thought. Liberals tend to put down any cultural force, such as television, which has not been anointed by some kind of special holy water which can only be conferred by the elites of Cambridge, Mass., and Manhattan. Rock is low-life and fascistic, but tennis elbow from playing in a court that cost $40 an hour in Manhattan is deeply "in." Television is

53

beneath discussing in serious terms, according to your really important liberals; but ballet and the opera, which can only be seen by the rich few and which the great mass of people find boring, are immensely significant.

I resent the liberals' belief that all American greatness began with JFK and ended with him.

I resent the liberals' idea that the average American is a savage.

I resent the constant liberal putdown of what is American and praise of what is foreign.

I resent the liberals' idea that great ideas always come from the big cities and that small towns are only suitable for summer homes, that the countryside is peopled by dolts looking to shoot every person with long hair that they see.

"I believe that there will be a desperate and crying need for the values of liberalism in the 1980's."

A Liberal Looks at the Eighties

Paul F. Tsongas

Paul E. Tsongas is the junior democratic senator from Massachusetts. A long-time champion of liberal causes and politics, Tsongas recently has been expressing concern over the future of liberalism in America. In the following viewpoint, originally delivered before the National Convention of Americans for Democratic Action, he addresses himself to that concern.

Consider the following questions while reading:
1. **What were some of the accomplishments of liberals during the 60's?**
2. **What are some of the causes of liberalism's difficulties today?**
3. **What can liberals do to prevent a conservative tidal wave in the 80's?**

Paul E. Tsongas. Excerpts from a speech delivered before the U.S. Senate. *Congressional Record*, Vol. 126, No. 98, June 16, 1980.

It is not popular these days to be a liberal. Every narrow, special interest in Washington is building and attacking our caricature. Liberals, supposedly, are the dreamers—idealogues making Rube Goldberg-type contraptions to regulate the citizen.

The facts refute this cartoon. In the last two decades, which shaped my own set of values, liberals have seen this Nation and the world as it was. We have made practical, realistic changes to make it work better.

THE LIBERAL 60's

Look at the civil rights movement, the great moral challenge of the 1960's. To us, equal opportunity is a crucial principle, but it battled inch by inch with other principles. Reactionaries fought a rearguard action, using the principles of States' rights and property rights. With the help of many people here today, it became an unequal contest. There was no way that this country could withstand the demand for equal rights. A house divided—by color—could not stand.

A NEW ERA

This is a different generation. And if we do not speak to this generation in its terms, liberalism will decline.

Senator Paul E. Tsongas, Democrat, Massachusetts

The principle was that we ought not remain divided; the reality was that we could not.

Look at the Great Society, which aimed to share growing U. S. prosperity among all our citizens. Health care, voting rights, job training, early schooling, and other social programs were pushed through the Congress to help make the ideal of equality a reality...

Look at the Peace Corps, an international expression of our commitment to human dignity. The Peace Corps is an expression of American principles — but the bottom line is that it works...

Look at the antiwar movement, a powerful rejection of the traditional cold war view that we would support repressive and corrupt regimes with our guns and our lives if only they would spout the necessary anti-Communist rhetoric...

The world of the 1960's was well-suited to the rationale of liberalism. At home, we marched to achieve a just society, then voted to build a great society. Abroad, we volunteered to serve peacefully, then marched against a war. To someone choosing a personal set of values in the 1960's, liberals were raising the important issues and working toward practical solutions.

FATEFUL CROSSROADS

Most of us here today remember those exciting years. But in a way, it is a shame that there are not more of you who do not — who are too young to have been participants or even observers. Fewer young people are joining the liberal cause in 1980 than in the 1960's. Our case seems less compelling now. We must look at the world with fresh eyes, and understand why.

The fact is that liberalism is at a crossroads. It will either evolve to meet the issues of the 1980's or it will be reduced to an interesting topic for Ph.D.-writing historians.

In part, liberalism's difficulties reflect a natural cycle of resentment and retrenchment against the gains of the 1960's and, yes, there were some in the 1970's, too. There is an anti-political, anti-Washington element that conservatives are exploiting. Many Americans are discouraged and confused about current problems in the economy and society. Conservative rhetoric is raising their hopes for a 20-mule-team march into the past.

If we are to mobilize a new generation to move forward with liberal leadership, we must understand that the average young American is just that—part of a new generation. A generation that never experienced the abuses and injustices that molded us. A generation that takes for granted the social equities that we had to fight for. In short, they have never known that anger that fed the liberal cause...

This is a different generation. And if we do not speak to this generation in its terms, liberalism will decline. And if we do not meet these needs, liberalism should decline...

THE CRITICAL EIGHTIES

If liberalism is to survive, it must have relevant answers to the critical problems of the '80s and must appeal to a whole new generation of Americans, who have never known the abuses and injustices that inspired the great liberal achievements of the New Deal, the Great Society, the civil rights movement.

Donald C. McKay, Jr., Delegate to the Americans for Democratic Action Convention, 1980.

MOVE TOWARD THE 80's

The fact is that I believe that liberalism must extricate itself from the 1960's when we had the answers. We must move on to the pressing problems of the 1980's, and we must have the answers that seem relevant and appropriate to the generation of potential liberals.

Some will argue that if we do not, it does not matter. Nonsense.

I believe that there will be a desperate and crying need for the values of liberalism in the 1980's.

This country is eagerly searching for solutions, and many are looking to Ronald Reagan for leadership. And Congress is increasingly sounding like Ronald Reagan.

This potential return to a cold-war mentality is unacceptable. Do we have to learn the lesson of Vietnam all over again?

This potential return to totally unfettered private enterprise is unacceptable. How many Love Canals are enough?

This potential return to racial benign neglect is unaccept-

58

able. How many times must a city burn before we re-awaken to the needs of our people...?

ORGY OF CONSERVATISM

We must respond. Because if we do not, we will leave the field to the champions of divisiveness. We will relinquish American leadership to those who are comfortable with exclusivity.

In an age of potential nuclear devastation, that prospect is not an academic one.

I, for one, do not wish that this world, this country — indeed, my family — be incinerated in an orgy of conservative, simplistic ideology.

We must provide the leadership if this country is to be man's last great hope.

"We are being prisoned by inflation and progressive tax rates."

A Conservative Looks at the Eighties

Jack Kemp

Jack Kemp (R-N.Y.) is a member of the U.S. House of Representatives. A noted conservative legislator, Kemp figured prominently as a possible vice-presidential running mate for Ronald Reagan in 1980. The following is taken from the keynote address delivered by Kemp at the annual meeting of the Conservative Political Action Conference held in February, 1980, in Washington, D.C. He was honored at the meeting with the "Conservative of the Year Award in the U.S. House of Representatives."

Consider the following questions while reading:
1. **According to Kemp, what is the central problem facing America today?**
2. **How would Kemp "reform" America's monetary system?**
3. **In your opinion, would Kemp's proposals result in a sound monetary system? Explain your answer.**

Jack Kemp. Keynote address delivered at the Seventh Annual Conservative Political Action Conference (CPAC).

Americans are demanding—begging for us to give them—what may be called a true and radical vision for the 1980's, radical in both dictionary senses of the word. First, "a departure from the usual or traditional," a departure from the orthodox range of policies which are causing our 13-percent inflation and unemployment which is rising toward 8 percent. And second, "relating to a root or origin," in the sense that what Americans want to conserve are the basic principles of economic and political freedom on which this country was founded, and without which we get the sort of mess we are in today...

The task before us is to put forward an agenda and vision for the 1980's which represents a consensus of the American people, not a coalition of interest groups...

We need an agenda for action which addresses the needs of all Americans, black and white, rich and poor, young and old, labor and capital...

THE PROBLEM TODAY

What is the central problem facing America? It is the combination, the collision, of inflation on the progressive federal tax system. This is a combination unprecedented in the history of our country, which is why I think for the first time in our history we are feeling our strength ebbing away, or self-confidence waning. More and more of our people feel pessimistic about their own futures, and the country itself no longer projects a national vitality to the rest of the world. And the Soviet Union behaves as if the United States has already been eclipsed as a global leader deserving of respect.

We are being poisoned by inflation and progressive tax rates. Inflation—a decline in the value of money—by itself is destructive. When savings melt away, our citizens are discouraged from working in order to save. We are encouraged to live in the present, narrowing instead of lifting our horizons. Progressivity in tax rates by itself discourages us from increasing our productive efforts as individuals, because the system progressively reduces the reward for our efforts. The combination of the two is horrendous! Even as inflation saps our ability to save for the future, to invest in our futures, it lifts us into higher progressive tax brackets that smother our incentive to work and produce...

But our agenda for the 1980's is not merely to limit the damage which inflation can wreak on Americans because of an outdated tax code. The next item on our agenda for the 1980's is a specific program to end inflation.

61

Inflation can only be conquered by straightening out our money. People don't cause inflation by putting up prices or bidding up labor. When they do, they are almost always defending themselves against the government, the real culprit.

A TAX REDUCTION

President John F. Kennedy was not generally considered a conservative, but he had his economics right in 1963, when he said, "If we were to slide into a recession through failure to act on taxes, the cash deficit for next year would be larger without the tax reduction than the estimated deficit with the tax reduction."

Jack Kemp, Republican, N.Y., House of Representatives

A RETURN TO GOLD

We must reform the monetary system and once again make the U. S. dollar as "good as gold." We have to move ahead toward a system that once again requires the government to redeem the paper dollars it prints with a precise, predictable amount of something of value. The discouraging inflation we are now experiencing really began in earnest when President Nixon cut the dollar's link with gold in 1971. He did so on the advice of economists who genuinely believed a cheaper dollar would improve American competitiveness. It has caused only inflation and grief, and the average citizen knows it.

The cause of inflation is no different today than it was 100 years ago or at any time in the history of money. Inflation is a decline in the monetary standard. Our forefathers maintained absolutely stable prices for more than 130 years—wholesale prices were the same in 1930 as in 1800—with little more than quill pens and parchment ledgers. Surely we can at least match their success, if not improve upon it.

The question is nothing more nor less than who shall control the creation of money—a government monopoly, or the people? With a fixed value for the dollar, the government is forced to create only as many or as few dollars as people demand. The government cannot both observe a monetary standard which maintains stable prices, and simultaneously engage in paper deflation or inflation.

A BALANCED BUDGET

Finally, there is the strategy for balancing the budget. John Anderson said recently that we can't cut tax rates, improve our defense and balance the budget without mirrors. This is basically the same argument that has governed budget-balancing strategies for the past 15 years or so: allow tax rates to increase as inflation pushes everyone into higher tax brackets. We've been waiting 15 years, and we haven't had a single year in which the national debt did not increase.

Those who oppose tax-rate reductions until the budget is balanced—that is, those who favor allowing tax rates to rise until the budget is balanced—are extremely shortsighted. The biggest savings to be made in the budget are in controlling the so-called "uncontrollables"—the transfer payments which constitute nearly half the budget and are affected primarily by the rates of inflation and unemployment. The cost of wasting the lives of 6 or 8 million idle Americans is the largest single item in the budget. Our budget-balancing strategy must be to end inflation and lower unemployment, not raise it.

President John F. Kennedy was not generally considered a conservative, but he had his economics right in 1963, when he said, "If we were to slide into a recession through failure to act on taxes, the cash deficit for next year would be larger without the tax reduction than the estimated deficit with the tax reduction. Indeed, a new recession could break all peacetime records." This is exactly the case in 1980...

Don Hesse © 1980, *St. Louis Globe-Democrat*. Reprinted with permission Los Angeles Times Syndicate.

THE POSSIBLE SOLUTIONS

This is the essence of my agenda for the 1980's...

First, it is a commitment to consensus, a program to be put forward by conservatives, but which represents a consensus of the country, not only a part of it. A specific proposal to represent this commitment is the national initiative.

Second, it is a commitment to end the collision between inflation and our progressive, outdated tax code, which is daily raising the tax on the effort, the productivity, the thrift, and the enterprise of all Americans. We must lower income tax rates across the board, and adjust all federal taxes automatically every year for inflation.

Third, it is a commitment to restore gold backing for the dollar. This government guarantee for the buying power of a dollar is the only monetary policy in history which has consistently maintained stable prices. Our problems with severe inflation began with the suspension of dollar convertibility into gold in March 1968, and accelerated with our official default on international debts in August 1971. Our economy will not be as "sound as a dollar" again until a dollar is as "good as gold."

Fourth, we need a new approach to the budget, which treats that document as it should be treated — as a blueprint for the demands on private production and the allocation of public resources in the coming year. What I am proposing Is nothing but gearing the nature of our federal budget to the needs of Americans, instead of the reverse...

I vividly recall the closing comments in Durant's *History of Civilization* on the death of Greek democracy: "The Assembly, a noble body in its better days, degenerated into a mob, rejecting all restraint, voting itself every favor, and taxing the people to the point of crushing their initiative, their industriousness and their thrift."

Our object in putting forth this agenda for the 1980's is not merely greater prosperity without inflation, but to preserve, protect and promote democracy in America...

Liberal Publications

The Christian Century
407 South Dearborn Street
Chicago, IL 60605

Published 43 times per year
$18.00 per year

The Humanist
7 Harwood Drive
Amherst, NY 14226

Published Bi-Monthly
$12.00 per year

The Nation
72 Fifth Avenue
New York, NY 10011

Published Weekly
$25.00 per year

The addresses and subscription rates of these periodicals are correct as of 1980.

The New Republic
P. O. Box 955
Farmingdale, NY 11737

Published Weekly
$28.00 per year

The Progressive
408 West Gorham Street
Madison, WI 53703

Published Monthly
$17.00 per year

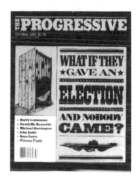

Sojourners
1309 L Street N.W.
Washington, DC 20005

Published Monthly
$12.00 per year

REVOLUTION AND CHANGE

The following exercise will explore your attitude toward change. Sometimes change brings progress, other times pain and suffering, and frequently both progress and human suffering and problems are by-products of social, political, scientific, and technological change. Change can occur slowly or it can come suddenly and quickly (revolutionary change).

PART I

Instructions

Consider each of the following circumstances carefully. Mark *G* whenever you feel gradual change is needed. Mark *R* for circumstances that you believe demand revolutionary change. And mark *S* if you think the status quo should be maintained (no change needed).

> R = Revolutionary Change
> G = Gradual Change
> S = Status Quo

_____ 1. U.S. energy policy

_____ 2. The Social Security System

_____ 3. Government's relationship to big business

_____ 4. U.S. foreign policy

_____ 5. Welfarism in the U.S.

_____ 6. A new strategic arms (SALT) agreement with Russia

_____ 7. The rights of gays

_____ 8. A new taxation structure

_____ 9. A more equitable sharing of the nation's wealth

_____ 10. Equal rights for women

_____ 11. Military expenditures by the federal government

_____ 12. Federal guidelines on air and water pollution

PART II

Instructions

STEP 1

The class should break into groups of four to six students.

STEP 2

Students should compare and discuss answers on each statement.

STEP 3

Each group then should choose a student to record the total number of R's, G's and S's within the group for each statement.

STEP 4

On the basis of these totals, the group should determine whether, as a group, it tends to be liberal, conservative or extremist.

STEP 5

The different class groups should then compare their respective totals and determine if the class as a whole tends to be liberal, conservative or extremist.

Chapter **3**

THE POLITICAL SPECTRUM

What is Conservatism?

"The vision of conservatism is one of common sense, practicality, and realism. It is concerned with the possible and the feasible."

What Conservatism Is

Jay A. Sigler

Jay A. Sigler is Professor of Political Science and Director of the Graduate Program in Public Policy at Rutgers University. He is the author of numerous scholarly articles and books including *Double Jeopardy, American Rights Policies* and *Courts and Public Policy.* In the following viewpoint, Professor Sigler offers a summary account of the conservative's views on human nature and government.

Consider the following questions while reading:

1. **List at least five distinguishing features of conservatism.**
2. **What is the conservative attitude toward government?**
3. **Do you believe that the conservative principles outlined in this viewpoint provide a sound basis for government? Explain your answer.**

Jay A. Sigler, *The Conservative Tradition in American Thought.* New York: G.P. Putnam's Sons, 1969. Copyright © by Educational Resources Corporation. Reprinted with permission of the publisher.

Conservatives do not have a rosy view of human nature. They are impressed by the frailty and weakness of man. The restraint of the evil tendencies of man is a proper object of government, but conservatives feel that the improvement of man is more the result of individual effort than it is of anything the state may do. Men do not change rapidly or easily. Governments and laws are not capable of making fundamental changes in the nature of man. The conservative accepts the mysterious uniqueness of man.

NATURE OF HUMANITY

The conservative suspicion of government flows from the same doubt about the good motives of men. Rulers, too, are fallible beings. Their plans and schemes may be motivated by selfishness, pride, or glory rather than by the common good.

The conservative prefers to emphasize the moral equality of men more than their legal, social, or economic equality. These latter equalities may be more superficial than moral equality and may also be antithetical to it.

The conservative accepts as natural the differences which separate men. Class, intelligence, nationality, and race make men different. Difference does not imply superiority or inferiority; it merely states an observable fact.

Conservatives have ingrained respect for talent and birth. The preference for the best man, rather than the most popular man, is a typical attitude. The aristocratic reformer is a familiar figure in American politics, especially in state and local politics. Open aristocratic preferences are rarely stated.

The conservative does not oppose change, but he does resist it. In the interest of social stability it is safer to retain a known constellation of relationships than blindly to seek new ones. Change must come, as it always has, but it can be guided by experience and fitted into the already existing patterns.

NATURE OF GOVERNMENT

Since government is to be distrusted, power must be diffused. Political power is inherently dangerous, so it must be controlled by dividing up responsibility, reducing authority. Arbitrary power is particularly odious, especially when wielded by an insensitive bureaucrat.

Government may promote morality, but it cannot produce universal prosperity. The government may assist the helpless, but only when they cannot help themselves, for to do so might destroy their individual self-respect.

INDIVIDUAL INITIATIVE

A conservative believes that, fundamentally, the individual is responsible for his own well-being, but that government should do those things for him that he can't do for himself. The liberal's first reaction to a problem is to ask: "How can government solve it?" The conservative first asks: "How can we help the individual solve it and should we?"

John J. Rhodes, Republican, Arizona, House of Representatives.

Freedom is not absolute or unconditional. Society creates duties as well as rights. Excessive selfishness is fed by insistence on personal rights at the cost of society itself. Men must learn to serve as well as to be served.

The Constitution provides the best guide to political action. It is an expression of the higher law which restricts arbitrary government. It is the symbol of the nation and the source of its stability.

Property has its rights, though these are not unlimited. The possession of private property is an asset for the society as well as for the possessors. Stability, work, and responsibility are encouraged by the system of private property.

THE CONSERVATIVE VISION

The vision of conservatism is one of common sense, practicality, and realism. It is concerned with the possible and the feasible. Reform is desirable, but only when it can succeed and when it really improves.

As can be seen, conservatism cannot be expressed in a set of programs, in a religious tract, or as a set of specific moral or political guides. In American politics it is a style rather than a creed. There is neither a monarchy nor an established religion to defend; only a Constitution and a historical method of practical, gradual change. Conservatism is a way of thinking and a way of speaking. The conservative is not sure that tomorrow will always be an improvement upon today or that "progress is our most important product." He doubts the wisdom of the current majority style, which happens to be liberalism. He offers the evidence of the history texts. There has been no Utopia in the past, and there will not be one in the future. In a phrase, the conservative is the man who is sure that he doesn't know the answers and doubts that you do.

"I know of no example in time or place of a society that has been marked by a large measure of political freedom, and that has not also used something comparable to a free market."

The Conservative View of Freedom

Milton Friedman

Milton Friedman is one of the leading and most influential defenders of traditional capitalism in the United States today. A winner of the Nobel Prize for economics in 1976, Friedman has authored several books supportive of conservative economic and political policies. His most recent work, *Free to Choose*, was written with his wife, Rose Friedman. In the following viewpoint, Friedman attempts to illustrate the relationship between economic and political freedom and concludes that they are inseparable.

Consider the following questions while reading:
1. **What is the dual role of economic arrangements in a free society?**
2. **According to Friedman, what should the role of government be in an economically free society?**
3. **Do you agree with Friedman's ideas on the relationship between economic and political freedom? Explain your answer.**

Milton Friedman, *Capitalism and Freedom*. Chicago: The University of Chicago Press, 1962. Reprinted from *Capitalism and Freedom* by Milton Friedman by permission of The University of Chicago Press.

It is widely believed that politics and economics are separate and largely unconnected; that individual freedom is a political problem and material welfare an economic problem; and that any kind of political arrangements can be combined with any kind of economic arrangements...

ROLE OF ECONOMICS

Economic arrangements play a dual role in the promotion of a free society. On the one hand, freedom in economic arrangements is itself a component of freedom broadly understood, so economic freedom is an end in itself. In the second place, economic freedom is also an indispensable means toward the achievement of political freedom.

Milton Friedman

The first of these roles of economic freedom needs special emphasis because intellectuals in particular have a strong bias against regarding this aspect of freedom as important. They tend to express contempt for what they regard as material aspects of life, and to regard their own pursuit of allegedly higher values as on a different plane of significance and as deserving of special attention. For most citizens of the country, however, if not for the intellectual, the direct importance of economic freedom is at least comparable in significance to the indirect importance of economic freedom as a means to political freedom.

The citizen of Great Britain, who after World War II was not permitted to spend his vacation in the United States because of exchange control, was being deprived of an essential freedom no less than the citizen of the United States, who was denied the opportunity to spend his vacation in Russia because of his political views. The one was ostensibly an economic limitation on freedom and the other a political limitation, yet there is no essential difference between the two...

FORCE OR COOPERATION

Viewed as a means to the end of political freedom, economic arrangements are important because of their effect on the concentration or dispersion of power. The kind of economic organization that provides economic freedom directly, namely, competitive capitalism, also promotes political freedom because it separates economic power from political power and in this way enables the one to offset the other.

Historical evidence speaks with a single voice on the relation between political freedom and a free market. I know of no example in time or place of a society that has been marked by a large measure of political freedom, and that has not also used something comparable to a free market to organize the bulk of economic activity...

Fundamentally, there are only two ways of co-ordinating the economic activities of millions. One is central direction involving the use of coercion — the technique of the army and of the modern totalitarian state. The other is voluntary co-operation of individuals — the technique of the market place.

The possibility of co-ordination through voluntary co-operation rests on the elementary — yet frequently denied — proposition that both parties to an economic transaction benefit from it, *provided the transaction is bi-laterally voluntary and informed.*

Exchange can therefore bring about co-ordination without coercion. A working model of a society organized through voluntary exchange is a *free private enterprise exchange economy*—what we have been calling competitive capitalism...

FREEDOM, FREEDOM, FREEDOM

One conservative principle is individual freedom to the maximum degree consistent with the freedom of others. Another is equality of opportunity. Another principle is economic freedom as represented by the private-enterprise system. Also, conservatives believe in a sufficiently strong defense to insure that we can maintain our freedoms and the economic system necessary to them.

Senator Robert Taft, Jr., Republican, Ohio.

WHAT ABOUT GOVERNMENT

So long as effective freedom of exchange is maintained, the central feature of the market organization of economic activity is that it prevents one person from interfering with another in respect of most of his activities. The consumer is protected from coercion by the seller because of the presence of other sellers with whom he can deal. The seller is protected from coercion by the consumer because of other consumers to whom he can sell. The employee is protected from coercion by the employer because of other employers for whom he can work, and so on. And the market does this impersonally and without centralized authority.

Indeed, a major source of objection to a free economy is precisely that it does this task so well. It gives people what they want instead of what a particular group thinks they ought to want. Underlying most arguments against the free market is a lack of belief in freedom itself.

The existence of a free market does not of course eliminate the need for government. On the contrary, government is essential both as a forum for determining the "rules of the game" and as an umpire to interpret and enforce the rules decided on. What the market does is to reduce greatly the range of issues that must be decided through political means, and thereby to minimize the extent to which government need participate directly in the game. The characteristic feature of action through political channels is that it tends to require or enforce substantial conformity. The great advantage of the market, on the other hand, is that it permits wide diversity. It is, in political terms, a system of proportional representation. Each man can vote, as it were, for the color of tie he wants and get it; he does not have to see what color the majority wants and then, if he is in the minority, submit.

"Human rights before property rights."

Reprinted with permission of *New Guard* magazine

It is this feature of the market that we refer to when we say that the market provides economic freedom. But this characteristic also has implications that go far beyond the narrowly economic. Political freedom means the absence of coercion of a man by his fellow men. The fundamental threat to freedom is power to coerce, be it in the hands of a monarch, a dictator, an oligarchy, or a momentary majority. The preservation of freedom requires the elimination of such concentration of power to the fullest possible extent and the dispersal and distribution of whatever power cannot be eliminated — a system of checks and balances. By removing the organization of economic activity from the control of political authority, the market eliminates this source of coercive power. It enables economic strength to be a check to political power rather than a reinforcement.

"Liberals have encouraged the notion that societies can make use of part of the wealth of their most fortunate members in order to abate hardships of their poorest."

The Liberal View of Freedom

Milton Viorst

Milton Viorst, the author of *Liberalism: A Guide to Its Past, Present and Future in American Politics*, is a noted journalist whose articles have appeared in major publications throughout the United States. In the following viewpoint, Viorst outlines the liberal's concept of freedom and compares it to that of the conservative.

Consider the following questions while reading:
1. According to Viorst, what are some of the differences between liberals and conservatives?
2. Why have liberals "constantly challenged the *status quo*?"
3. What are the differences between Viorst's and Friedman's concepts of freedom?

Milton Viorst, *Liberalism: A Guide to Its Past, Present and Future in American Politics*. New York: Avon Books, 1963. Reprinted with permission of the author.

To the liberal, freedom is the pinnacle of human values. His belief in it is immutable. It is, in itself, the worthiest of ends. But, equally important, without it the destiny of the nation would become fixed. The liberal can tolerate many injustices as long as he knows he is free to seek redress. In the absence of freedom, government becomes the agent of the *status quo*, the servant of the past, a silent accomplice to social stagnation. Freedom is the vehicle of change, which the liberal considers essential to the survival of a dynamic society...

POLITICAL FREEDOM AND TYRANNY

The liberal's concept of freedom must not be mistaken for the conservative's, however. In exalting the principle of freedom, each gives it a different meaning. When the nation was founded, it seemed to the Founding Fathers that freedom was indivisible...

LIBERALISM PROTECTS CONSERVATISM

The true conservative seeks to protect the system of private property and free enterprise by correcting such injustices and inequalities as arise from it. The most serious threat to our institutions comes from those who refuse to face the need for change. Liberalism becomes the protection for the far-sighted conservative.

Franklin D. Roosevelt, September 30, 1936.

Though the Founding Fathers believed in economic freedom, they realized that political freedom was the only obstacle to tyranny. Without it, the abuse of power, no matter what its nature, might go unchecked. But conservatives have reversed the order of priority. Demoting political freedom, they have elevated economic freedom to first place in the hierarchy of society's values.

WHAT IS FREEDOM?

Conservatives consider freedom the right to go into business, to make profit, to spend and invest, to negotiate contracts, all without restriction. They recognize that to deter the unscrupulous, law must impose some regulation on these activities. Some concede the need for more regulation, some call for less. In their extreme form, conservatives conceive of freedom as the right to plunder. More often, they consider laws that go beyond simple police functions to be restrictions of freedom. Taxes, in this view, are threats to freedom. Social security, pure food and drug laws, farm production quotas, industrial safety standards are all impositions on freedom. Many consider labor unions to be in conflict with freedom. Government's role, according to the responsible conservative, is to encourage the maximum amount of economic freedom compatible with the preservation of society.

The liberal, on the other hand, considers freedom the right to speak, to write, to hold meetings, to form parties, to dissent from conventional opinion. Because he is committed to improving the lot of the distressed, he is a staunch defender of the means inherent within the Constitution for giving effect to new theories, innovations, social improvements. He is frequently irritated at the frustrations of constitutional government which permit conservatives to delay measures he considers overdue and defeat others that he deems essential. But he has learned that the mechanism for change does exist. This mechanism has its basis in political freedom...

SOCIAL JUSTICE

In recent history, societies have moved in the direction of reducing the grossest economic disparities between their members. Liberals have applauded this development. They have worked for it as an objective that they consider vital for a free civilization. They believe deeply in equalizing opportunities, eliminating fear and insecurity, guaranteeing decent standards of living. Liberals have encouraged the notion that societies can, by lawful methods, make use of part of the wealth of their most fortunate members in order to abate the hardships of their poorest. They have, in brief, elevated the principle of social justice above the principle of economic freedom in their hierarchy of values.

This has meant that liberals have constantly challenged the *status quo*. It has meant that they have had to take on in the political arena the conservative seeking to protect his property. The liberal has invoked political freedom in his struggle to upset the *status quo*. The conservative has cited economic freedom in his struggle to maintain it...

THE TWO FREEDOMS

The priority of the two freedoms, economic and political, has often been the subject of dispute in the courts. In 1922, a very conservative judge declared that, "of the three funda-

PEOPLE BEFORE THINGS

Liberalism to me is an allegiance to people rather than to things and abstract principles. In any situation, the human factors are most important. Nations are judged, and they will progress, by virtue of how they take care of the weak and lowly — to see that they have money and opportunity. Normal free enterprise will allow the powerful to get their share, but large profits don't trickle down to the poor.

Andrew Young, Former U. S. Ambassador to the U. N.

mental principles which underlie government and for which government exists, the protection of life, liberty and property, the chief of these is property." But in 1949, Supreme Court Justice Frankfurter stated that, "those liberties of the individual which history has attested as the indispensable conditions of an open as against a closed society come to this Court with a momentum for respect lacking when appeal is made to liberties which derive merely from shifting economic arrangements."

The conservative orientation toward property serves to explain why conservatives are normally the assailants when political freedoms are under attack. Throughout American history, the most serious violations against political liberty have always been committed by conservatives against those seeking, in one form or another, to upset the *status quo* in the distribution of property. The past quarter century has demonstrated again how deeply the commitment of liberals to civil liberties differs from that of conservatives.

*"Neo-conservatism affirms the tradi-
tional American idea of equality, but
rejects egalitarianism as a proper
goal for government to pursue."*

What is
Neo-conservatism?

Irving Kristol

Irving Kristol is a prominent editorialist whose pieces have
appeared in leading magazines and journals in the United
States. A professor of Urban Values at New York University
and Editor–in–Chief of *The Public Interest*, Kristol outlines
below what he considers to be the principle tenets of neo
(new)–conservatism.

Consider the following questions while reading:
1. **What are the differences between a neo–conservative
   and a liberal?**
2. **According to Kristol, what are the tenets of neo-
   conservatism?**

Irving Kristol, "What Is a Neo-Conservative?", *Newsweek*, January 19, 1976.
Copyright © 1976, by Newsweek, Inc. All Rights Reserved. Reprinted by
permission.

WHAT IS NEO-CONSERVATISM?

There can be no doubt that the political tendency deemed neo-conservative does exist, that it is represented in such journals as *The Public Interest* and *Commentary*, that it has become quite influential of late in shaping political attitudes in intellectual and academic circles, and that its views have even infiltrated the world of media and government. But it is also true that it is only a tendency, not a clearly defined "movement," that there is much heterogeneity in it, and that to those who do not closely follow intellectual controversy in America the term "conservative" can be misleading.

Let me see, therefore, if I can briefly outline the substance beneath the label, the vague consensus that seems to affiliate men and women who are frequently not even aware that they are part of a tendency, much less a neo-conservative one. It's a real enough thing we are talking about—I am not disputing that. But, at the moment, it needs describing more than it needs naming.

THE WELFARE STATE

1. Neo-conservatism is not at all hostile to the idea of a welfare state, but it is critical of the Great Society version of this welfare state. In general, it approves of those social reforms that, while providing needed security and comfort to the individual in our dynamic, urbanized society, do so with a minimum of bureaucratic intrusion in the individual's affairs. Such reforms would include, of course, social security, unemploy-

TIME FOR CONSERVATISM

The familiar call for government to rush to the rescue has died, even in the throats of the liberals themselves...

And step by step with the return of conservative attitudes on domestic issues we are seeing a hardening of popular sentiment in regard to foreign affairs as well. Public support for bigger defense expenditures is on the rise, and the "Vietnam code" of withdrawal and defeatism is a thing of the past. America hardly expects the future to be glorious, but it is at least getting serious about surviving.

William A. Rusher, *Human Events*, January 12, 1980.

ment insurance, some form of national health insurance, some kind of family-assistance plan, etc. In contrast, it is skeptical of those social programs that create vast and energetic bureaucracies to "solve social problems." In short, while being for the welfare state, it is opposed to the paternalistic state. It also believes that this welfare state will best promote the common good if it is conceived in such a way as not to go bankrupt.

2. Neo-conservatism has great respect—it is fair to say it has learned to have great respect—for the power of the market to respond efficiently to economic realities while preserving the maximum degree of individual freedom. Though willing to interfere with the market for overriding social purposes, it prefers to do so by "rigging" the market, or even creating new markets, rather than by direct bureaucratic controls. Thus it is more likely to favor housing vouchers for the poor than government-built low-income projects.

TRADITION AND CHANGE

3. Neo-conservatism tends to be respectful of traditional values and institutions: religion, the family, the "high culture" of Western civilization. If there is any one thing that neo-conservatives are unanimous about, it is their dislike of the "counter-culture" that has played so remarkable a role in American life over these past fifteen years. Neo-conservatives are well aware that traditional values and institutions do change in time, but they prefer that such change be gradual and organic. They believe that the individual who is abruptly "liberated" from the sovereignty of traditional values will soon find himself experiencing the vertigo and despair of nihilism. Nor do they put much credence in the notion that individuals can "create" their own values and then incorporate them into a satisfying "life-style." Values emerge out of the experience of generations and represent the accumulated wisdom of these generations; they simply cannot be got out of rap sessions about "identity" or "authenticity."

EQUALITY VS EGALITARIANISM

4. Neo-conservatism affirms the traditional American idea of equality, but rejects egalitarianism—the equality of condition for all citizens—as a proper goal for government to pursue. The equality proclaimed by the Declaration of Independence is an equality of natural rights—including the right to become unequal (within limits) in wealth, or public esteem, or influence. Without *that* right, equality becomes the enemy

Weighing in

Reprinted with permission from the *Minneapolis Tribune*.

of liberty. To put it in more homely terms: the encouragement of equality of opportunity is always a proper concern of democratic government. But it is a dangerous sophistry to insist that there is no true equality of opportunity unless and until everyone ends up with equal shares of everything.

AMERICAN FOREIGN POLICY

5. In foreign policy, neo-conservatism believes that American democracy is not likely to survive for long in a world that is overwhelmingly hostile to American values, if only because our transactions (economic and diplomatic) with foreign nations are bound eventually to have a profound impact on our own domestic economic and political system. So neo-conservatives are critical of the post-Vietnam isolationism now so popular in Congress, and many are suspicious of "detente" as well. On specific issues of foreign policy, however, the neo-conservative consensus is a weak one. In the case of Vietnam, neo-conservatives went every which way.

So there it is—oversimplified but not, I think, distorted. Not all neo-conservatives will accept all of those tenets; but most will accept most of them. Is neo-conservatism the right label for this constellation of attitudes? I don't mind it—but then, if the political spectrum moved rightward, and we should become "neo-liberal" tomorrow, I could accept that too. As a matter of fact, I wouldn't be too surprised if just that happened.

"If the best neo-conservatives can offer is a return to some semi-feudal system of privilege...then they, and we, are indeed lost."

A Critique of Neo-Conservatism

Isidore Silver

Isidore Silver is a professor of constitutional law and history at John Jay College of Criminal Justice (The City University of New York). In the following viewpoint originally entitled "What Flows from Neo-Conservatism", Silver levels a multi-sided attack at neo-conservative political philosophy.

Consider the following questions while reading:
1. According to the author, what are some of the flaws in neo-conservative thought?
2. Why does Silver feel that neo-conservatism can be disastrous for the United States?

Isidore Silver, "What Flows from Neo-Conservatism," *The Nation*, July 9, 1977. Copyright 1977 *Nation* magazine, The Nation Associates, Inc.

Neo-Conservatism is a philosophy of public affairs that emphasizes the necessity for orderly economic reform, that recognizes a greater governmental role in effecting change than traditional conservatives would allow, and that claims to be pragmatic in assessing the costs and benefits of recent reforms. It casts a baleful eye on the New Frontier's attempt to redistribute political power, and winces at any public effort to do more than place an economic floor under poverty. Thus, Neo-Conservatives appear to be mildly liberal in domestic policy.

Foreign policy is another matter. Neo-Conservatives staunchly support democracy (especially Israel's), but reluctantly concede that most of the world is non- or anti-democratic. Any distaste for local dictatorships is subordinated to pragmatic considerations of the national interest—i.e., are those countries our allies in the war against communism? While eschewing "morals" in foreign policy, Neo-Conservatives espouse two nonpragmatic duties of the United States—Israel must be preserved and protected and Soviet Jews must be free to dissent or, if necessary, emigrate. Only a militarily powerful America can achieve these goals...

UNEARNED PRIVILEGE

Neo-Conservatives recognize the strength of the notion of equality in American life. They are wary of it because it can be transformed (by liberals) into the notion of what Irving Kristol has called "egalitarianism." Kristol finds the latter—"the equality of condition for all citizens"—antithetical to liberty, including the "right to become unequal." It is government's duty to provide a floor, even an ever rising floor, to those less fortunate or less gifted, but not to "level" everyone else down so that the floor becomes a ceiling.

"Liberty" thus becomes the liberty to rise by means of natural talent beyond the circumstances and station of one's birth. Government's duty is to recognize, protect and even encourage that ability. While that proposition, stated as an ideal, is hardly controversial, there may be considerable doubt about its purity in political society, especially a political society featuring modern versions of unearned privilege. Neo-Conservatives oppose not privilege, just unearned privilege...

NEED FOR ABUNDANCE

Neo-Conservatives do not see equality and liberty in continual interaction. Their perspective blinds them to issues that do not fall within their conceptual framework. *Commentary* and *The Public Interest* do not run pieces on the role of the corporation in American life, the weakness of even the Meany labor movement as an economic force, or a multitude of problems about power in the society. Rather, their truncated vision presupposes an economically abundant society which can expand to meet the inevitable demands of the safely channeled labor movement. Perhaps, for some Neo-Conservatives, a romantic socialism is still in the distant future; pending that, they will continue to make alliances to shore up the (always) sagging buttresses.

They will also continue to lecture the American people on the need to curb political and economic appetites, to instill such virtues as respect for authority, and to preach that things are not as bad as radicals (or even liberals) keep telling them. As critics, they are superb — they will continue to point out the failures of welfare-state liberalism. As preachers, they may be less successful for the history of corporate America has been a story of voracious appetite, disrespect for authority (at least governmental authority) and a Lockean insistence on the rights of property. The corporation has taught us all the vices derided by the Neo-Conservatives — including the artful manipulation of government for private ends. Power holders no more believe in a "public philosophy" than do power seekers.

Since Neo-Conservatism, if its public message is to succeed at all, depends upon economic abundance...an end to abundance will present critical problems...

NEO-CONSERVATISM CONFUSION

The neo-conservative believes not chiefly in principles but in empirical techniques...this approach means that the neo-conservative usually cannot tell you what is wrong with social programs until they have already been entrenched and done their damage. Then the neo-conservative will tell you that these programs are part of the very fabric of our political culture and cannot be repealed. What use is that?

George Gilder, Author of *Sexual Suicide, On the Rocks* and *Visible Man.*

"WE ARE LOST"

Ironically, the Neo-Conservative world view has depended upon the liberal "interest group politics" it now deplores, and should those politics pass, the Neo-Conservative will be bailing in the same leaky boat with the American liberal...

As Neo-Conservatism struggles with its paradox, we must struggle with ours. Can the promise of a democratic society be fulfilled by an economic and political system that sanctions vast private power and wealth along with considerable public poverty ("middle-class" as well as "lower-class" poverty)? If the economic pie does not continue to grow, what kind of struggle will ensue? If social disorder, as manifested in crime, drugs, divorce and a host of other indicators, continues to spiral, will repression work or will the causes be seen as systemic? How can the cities be restored and at what cost? Who will bear the cost?

If Neo-Conservatives continue to grapple with symptoms — and not very imaginatively, at that — rather than causes, if their considerable intelligence and critical abilities become increasingly simple-minded, if their preoccupation with the dangers of Populism and equality become increasingly irrelevant to our real problems, then the society has lost. If the alliance with traditional conservatives solidifies into a simplistic defense of the precarious status quo, then the social calamity so feared by the Neo-Conservatives may well come to pass. If the best the Neo-Conservatives can offer is a return to some semi-feudal system of privilege and a disillusionment with the democratic promise, then they, and we, are indeed lost.

Conservative Publications

Christianity Today
465 Gundersen Drive
Carol Stream, IL 60187

Published Bi-Monthly
$18.00 per year

Commentary
165 East 56th Street
New York, NY 10022

Published Monthly
$24.00 per year

Conservative Digest
631 Independence Ave.
Marion, OH 43302

Published Monthly
$15.00 per year

The addresses and subscription rates of these periodicals are correct as of 1980.

Human Events
422 First Street, S.E.
Washington, DC 20003

Published Weekly
$25.00 per year

National Review
150 East 35th Street
New York, NY 10016

Published Bi -Weekly
$24.00 per year

New Guard
Young American for Freedom
Woodland Road
Sterling, VA 22170

Published Monthly
$5.00 per year

Vital Speeches
City News Publishing Company
Box 606
Southold, NY 11971

Published Bi-Weekly
$18.00 per year

DISTINGUISHING BETWEEN FACT AND OPINION

This discussion activity is designed to promote experimentation with one's ability to distinguish between fact and opinion. Consider the following example. If an ultra-liberal individual is elected president of the United States at some future date, that would be a fact. However, whether or not the United States would be better off socially, economically and politically with an ultra-liberal president is a matter of opinion. Future historians will agree that the individual in question *was* a president of the United States. But even their interpretations of the political significance of his or her administration probably will vary greatly.

PART I

Instructions

Some of the following statements are taken from this book and some have other origins. Consider each statement carefully. Mark *O* for any statement you feel is an opinion or interpretation of facts. Mark *F* for any statement you believe is a fact. Then discuss and compare your judgments with those of other class members.

O = Opinion
F = Fact

_____ 1. In the 1960's, liberals were raising the important issues and working toward practical solutions.

_____ 2. There will be a desperate and crying need for the values of liberalism in the 1980's.

_____ 3. These days, more and more American people feel pessimistic about their own futures, and the country itself no longer projects a national vitality to the rest of the world.

_____ 4. People don't cause inflation by putting up prices or bidding up labor. The spending habits of big government is the real cause of inflation.

_____ 5. In 1980, Ronald Reagan was elected president of the United States.

_____ 6. No one is anyone else's master, and no one is anyone else's slave.

_____ 7. For anyone — including government — to attempt to limit my freedom to do as I please is to violate my rights.

_____ 8. Generally speaking, conservatives tend to support big business while liberals tend to support labor.

_____ 9. Inflation lessens the value of the dollar.

_____ 10. Anarchy — that is the absence of government and laws — will lead to the highest form of individual freedom.

_____ 11. In a state of Anarchy, the strong will prey upon the weak.

_____ 12. Politically and economically, the United States is moving toward a socialistic, welfare state.

PART II

Instructions

STEP 1

The class should break into groups of four to six students.

STEP 2

Each small group should try to locate two statements of fact and two statements of opinion in this book.

STEP 3

Each group should choose a student to record its statements.

STEP 4

The class should discuss and compare the small groups' statements.

Chapter

THE POLITICAL SPECTRUM

What is Extremism?

"Violence, deceit and the total disregard for the civil liberties of others are just some of the extremist measures employed by both the far right and left."

What Extremism Is

David L. Bender and Bruno Leone

Depending on one's point of view, a political idea may or may not be considered extreme. For that reason, extremism is perhaps the most difficult term on the political spectrum to define. We have chosen to deal with extremism as falling into two categories. In this viewpoint, we attempt to outline both categories and then elaborate upon the first or more radical variety.

Consider the following questions while reading:
1. Do you agree with the editors' idea, namely, that extremism falls into "very radical" and "less radical" categories?
2. List several characteristics which the far left and right have in common. List several characteristics which are distinct to each.

It is difficult to read or hear the phrase "a political extremist" without thinking of wild radicals shouting destructive slogans and intent upon the forcible overthrow of an established political system. By definition, an extremist is one "who holds extreme or advanced views or advocates extreme measures."* Yet significantly, this definition contains broader implications. "Extreme or advanced views" need not be destructive views. In fact, they may ultimately prove beneficial and acceptable to a society. They simply may be considered extremist because, for a time, they are beyond the fringes of majority opinion.

During the Colonial period in American history, for example, advocates of political independence were viewed as extremists. (This view was held not only by the British but also by many colonists themselves.) However once independence was achieved, the label "extremist" no longer applied. Yesterday's heresy had become today's orthodoxy.

Two Categories of Extremism

Recognizing that different wings of "extremism" may play a visible part in any nation's political life, the editors of this book have chosen to face the difficult question, What Is Extremism? in the following way. We will deal with extremism as falling into two categories. Further on in this viewpoint, we have outlined a series of principles which we believe to be representative of one category, namely the far right and left wing extremist groups in America. (The National Socialist White Peoples Party and the Communist Party, USA, typify such extremist groups.) These groups, and others like them, are characterized by certain common features. For one, they are experiencing terminal disenchantment with the nation's existing political system. Moreover, they are almost totally out of touch with the dominant values of the overwhelming majority of American citizens. Finally, their methods include violence, their propaganda promotes strife and their ideologies create national divisions.

The remaining five viewpoints in chapter four deal with what we perceive to be a far less virulent form of extremism. These viewpoints represent ideas which, although not a part of America's political mainstream, nonetheless contain elements which are not totally foreign to it. So why label them extremist? Because the essential and basic beliefs expressed in these viewpoints place them, at best, on the margins of the nation's political life.

*Websters New World Dictionary of the American Language

100

Libertarianism offers a good example of this latter brand of extremism. Some of the Libertarian party's programs (lower or no taxes, no foreign involvements) are those with which a majority of Americans can relate to and even sympathize with. However as a political philosophy or party, libertarianism appears to be exerting virtually no visible or direct influence upon America's foreign and domestic policies. Although libertarians boast of being the third largest political party in the United States, numerically (in terms of a partisan following), they are far outdistanced by the Democratic and Republican majorities. In a position paper published prior to the 1974 congressional elections, the party stated that its goal was "to become a major political force in the United States by 1980." Yet despite the dissatisfaction of the American electorate with the two major party candidates in the 1980 presidential election, there were no large defections to the Libertarian candidate, Ed Clark. Many libertarians are now claiming that within a decade, the Libertarian party will be one of two major parties in the United States. If that claim proves true and the libertarians do achieve a major party status by 1990, then the extremist label will stand corrected.

The Common Characteristics of Far Left and Right Extremists

The following outlines those features typical of far right and left wing extremist groups in America. However, before looking at the characteristics that are peculiar to the right and left respectively, it would be helpful to consider some characteristics which they have in common.

1. **Extreme measures.** Both recommend extreme measures in dealing with domestic and world problems as they tend to divide the world into the forces of good and evil. Evil, therefore, must be dealt with forcefully and immediately. The art of compromise, upon which the American system of government is founded, and a practice much used by mainstream liberals and conservatives, is derided as giving in to evil forces whether it be the forces of communism or the establishment.

2. **The Anti-Movement.** Related to the first characteristic of dividing the world into two opposing forces is the tendency to be "anti" something. This tendency may take the form of anti-communism, anti-Semitism, anti-U.N., anti-black, or anti-white. Indeed, the life giving power for many of these groups is their hatred or fear of some racial group, governmental agency or movement in society to which they attribute a great number if not all of society's problems.

3. **A Tendency to Disregard Civil Liberties and Laws in the Name of the Cause.** Because they are convinced of the purity of their cause and the evilness of those they oppose, they often feel justified in using drastic means to achieve their goals. Violence, deceit and the total disregard for the civil liberties of others are just some of the extreme measures employed by both right and left. The furthering of their cause rises above all other considerations.

Characteristics of the Far Right

1. An avid anti-communist sentiment, directed at communists within the United States and those abroad, is one of the most noticeable features of the far right. For the greater part of this century, the far right has felt that American government and society have been under covert attack by communists who have been quite successful in influencing American foreign and domestic policy.

2. Many far right organizations are openly anti-black, anti-Semitic and anti-Catholic.

3. The far right is concerned about the decline of traditional moral values. Many members of the far right belong to fundamentalist religious denominations which hold that declining morality in America is largely responsible for America's decline in world influence.

4. Far' right groups label as communist inspired movements, programs and organizations they are opposed to whether it be the civil rights movement, flouridation of city water or the American Civil Liberties Union.

5. The far right is concerned about the corrupting influence of the United States Supreme Court on American society. Indeed, it has been preaching for years about the intimate role of the Supreme Court in the international communist conspiracy.

6. The United Nations is seen as a socialistic tool, being used by the communists to enslave the world, and they urge the United States government to withdraw from it.

7. The far right opposes numerous government programs, alleging that the less the government does the harder it will be for the communists to take over.

8. The far right favors a rigid capitalistic system as opposed to any form of socialism.

Characteristics of the Far Left

The far left has changed its complexion considerably during the decades of the 1960's and 1970's. Daniel Boorstin presents a clear picture of pre-1960 members of the extremist left.

> *The Depression Decade beginning in 1929 saw in the United States a host of radicalisms, perhaps more numerous and more influential than any earlier period of our history. Many of these were left-wing movements, which included large numbers of our academics, intellectuals, and men of public conscience who became members or fellow travelers of groups dominated by Marxist ideas. They favored a reconstruction of American life on a base of socialism or communism. They had a great deal to do with promoting a new and wider American labor movement, with helping F.D.R. popularize the need for a welfare state, and with persuading Americans to join the war to stop Hitler. Although they fenced in American social scientists by new orthodoxies, they did have a generally tonic effect on American society. However misguided were many of the policies they advocated, these radicals did awaken and sensitize the American conscience. They confronted Americans with some facts of life which had been swept under the rug.* *

Boorstin claims that the radicals of the past were identified by three characteristics: (1) A search for some kind of new meaning whether in religious, social or economic programs. (2) A "specific content", a philosophy, a program, etc. (3) An allegiance to a common cause and an improvement of American society (an affirmation of community as Boorstin puts it).

The far left of the present is identified by different traits than those of the past.

1. Far left wing groups advocate a rigid socialist form of economy. Most of them believe that this will be achieved only by revolutionary means.

2. Members of the far left are driven by a sense of idealism that permits few compromises and generates a feeling of elitism.

*Daniel J. Boorstin, "The New Barbarians", *Esquire*, October, 1968, p. 159.

3. The far left is not concerned about the communist menace that troubles the far right and would point out that before Americans can condemn communists out of hand they must first solve their own domestic problems. Indeed, many in the far left are communists themselves.

4. The far left advocates "participatory democracy" which means that workers, students, the poor and minorities should participate directly in making decisions that affect them.

5. The far left identifies with neither the Republican nor the Democratic party.

6. Ideological differences often prevent unity among far leftists and hence one finds many left wing political organizations.

The characteristics of the far left and far right that have been listed are general characteristics. They may not apply to all radical extremist organizations but they should provide some insight into the philosophical and operational traits that make them uniquely different.

This viewpoint was meant to offer guidelines which will help the reader interpret the remaining viewpoints in this chapter. Hopefully, it also will furnish the reader with some understanding of the complex topic of political extremism.

"Socialist institutions...aim at humanity, fraternity, and equality — goals strikingly different from those of capitalism."

Socialism in America—The Political Left

Harold Freeman

Harold Freeman is a professor at the Massachusetts Institute of Technology where he has taught for over 45 years. The following viewpoint was taken from his book, *Toward Socialism in America*. In the reading, Freeman attempts to demonstrate the moral superiority of socialism over American capitalism.

Consider the following questions while reading:

1. **Do you agree with Freeman's criticism of capitalism? Explain your answer.**
2. **What are the basic assumptions upon which socialism is built?**
3. **List some of the goals of socialism.**

Harold Freeman, *Toward Socialism in America*. Cambridge: Schenkman Publishing Company, 1979. Reprinted with permission of the publisher.

Simple and attractive as basic socialist principles may turn out to be, it will probably not be they but rather the profound senselessness of capitalism that will continue to strip it of support...

FLAWS OF CAPITALISM

It is difficult to tolerate a man-made system whose behavior the men who made and direct it cannot predict, whose behavior a year ahead with respect to such important measures as employment, output, prices, and even stability has become a matter of conjecture, with as many "experts" predicting rise as fall, growth as decline, with government speaking for months and even years of "bottoming out," while academics suggest that "we tighten our belts" and business analysts report, with exemplary confidence, that "the economy may go either way..."

SOCIALISM MEANS FREEDOM

For individuals, socialism means an end to economic insecurity and exploitation. It means workers cease to be commodities bought and sold on the labor market, and forced to work as appendages to tools owned by someone else. It means a chance to develop all individual capacities and potentials within a free community of free individuals.

The People, An editorial, August 23, 1980.

It is a grim experience to put up with a system which, to survive, must periodically destroy the lives of a substantial number of the people in it. The day may come when the American people begin seriously to wonder why there *ever* need be bad times, why factories which are open this month must close the next; why food, goods, and medicine which are within income one year must be beyond it another; why thousands who work today must be idle tomorrow. If masses of people begin to reflect on these events, events which are conventional features of our economy, which provide fortunes for a few and misfortunes for many, and for which grown men and women can give no sensible justification, it may be the moment of dangerous truth for American capitalism...

SOCIALIST PRINCIPLES

Socialism begins with certain assumptions. First, that we are fraternal people. That we want to share love, share well-being, share power, that we want human dignity to prevail. That we have or can have fraternal goals. To these are added the beliefs that the desire to own anything privately is not "human nature," but rather, human nature historically conditioned by early capitalism, that the desire to own everything privately is a peculiar by-product of advanced capitalism.

Socialist institutions therefore aim at humanity, fraternity, and equality—goals strikingly different from those of capitalism. Socialism imagines that people are willing, perhaps even eager, to participate in the planning and activity which will permit us to approach these goals—rather than wait for them to eventuate, via an invisible hand, as an accidental by-product of a system which hardly acknowledges their existence. Socialist society will probably classify people by performance, as does capitalism, but what is meant by performance will be different; it will be performance toward fraternal goals...

SOCIALISM MEANS RESHAPING

Since socialists assume that human nature emerges from the kind of society in which we live, they argue that the highest freedom is not simply the ability to take one's place on the social ladder, but the opportunity to assume control over and constantly reshape the basic institutions of society.

John Buell and Tom DeLuca, *The Progressive*, March, 1977.

Production shall be publicly owned, and each person shall have the guaranteed right to participate in its activity and its proceeds, from birth through education, employment, retirement, to death. Marx viewed public ownership and the continuous right to participate in production as the means of ending alienation from the work we do, from the products we make, from the environment in which we live, from each other, and from ourselves. Making a living must also be living. Elements critical to the quality of life such as a sense of belonging, creativity, a capacity for reflection, the expression of talent, the satisfaction of needs, understanding, planning and deciding, and self-esteem must be built into the work we do. This is a critical principle of socialism, and it is the precise opposite of the principle of advanced capitalism which separates ownership and labor, strives for impersonality and anonymity in production, substitutes consumption for personal development, and in no way guarantees participation.

A second principle of socialism is generalized equality. Equality between sexes, among racial groups, equality in opportunity, equality in wealth and income. It is a generalized democratic principle contrasting with the narrow democracy of capitalism which merely permits people to choose among close variants of inequality...

HUMANITY FIRST

It is correct to say that the goal of socialism is humanity. In Marx, socialism is not fulfillment; it is only the basis, the condition for fulfillment. It is the springboard to the goals of self-development and self-realization. To achieve these goals, we argue that people must abandon a system which has neither love for them nor even any serious interest in them as people, a system which uses them simply as agents in a drive for private profit. It is a system which cannot be truthful for there is profit in deceit, it cannot be equitable for there is profit in discrimination.

"I react to those who advocate The Pill instead of purity, and demonstrations instead of dedication, and desire over discipline."

"I am a Reactionary" —The Political Right

Patricia Young

A Canadian, Patricia Young has written extensively and favorably on right-wing politics. In the following viewpoint, she reacts against political liberalism and social permissiveness. Young implies that a return to the values of the past would benefit America greatly.

Consider the following questions while reading:
1. **Why does the author call herself a reactionary?**
2. **Do you agree with her statements? Please explain your answer.**

Patricia Young, "I Am a Reactionary," *Life Lines*, Vol. 14, No. 63, May 29, 1972.

Just for the record — and without apology — I am a reactionary! I react to sin and sadism, riots and revolution, gutlessness and Godlessness; to philosophies and sophistries which seek to destory those values which make a country great, and which fashioned the very fabric of civilized mankind.

GOD AND THE DEVIL

I react to dancing the permissive polka with those who would whirl me all the way to Hell while whispering that "God is dead" and that the Devil is nothing but a myth. Yes, I am a reactionary: I react to those ministers who would convert my church into a hootenanny hall or a political forum.

Yes, I am a reactionary. I react to the emasculation of my Faith in the name of humanistic togetherness; I react to those who would seek to destroy my love for the Holy Bible, and my loyalty to the flag, and my esteem for the police.

I react to charges that I am personally guilty for other people's failures — as if I personally poured liquor down the alcoholic's throat, or peddled the heroin, or mugged a little old lady, or created the slums, or invented The Bomb!

I react to the glorification of the welfare state as a substitute for working for a living. I react to stupid kids who turn to pot and run away from pink lemonade. Yes, indeed, I am a reactionary! I react to those who advocate The Pill instead of purity, and demonstrations instead of dedication, and desire over discipline, selfishness instead of sacrifice. I react to those who constantly prate about "rights" but who don't give a darn what's right.

THE RADICAL LEFT

I react to the portrayal of my friends in America as "Fascist beasts," and to those who regard Communist dictators as Santa Claus. I react to those who consider love as nothing more than sex, and who contend that "art" is a film showing an unmarried couple in bed together. Yes, sir, I react to student radicals who are so enamored by their own worth that they must destroy all other worths — who are for nothing except their "right" to be against everything.

I'm a reactionary, yes I am: I react to the stupid sentimentality of amateur do-gooders who, like carved wooden monkeys, see no evil, speak no evil, and hear no evil — even

LIBERAL ENEMY LIST

1. MIDDLE-CLASS, MIDDLE-AGED, MIDDLE-INCOME MIDDLE-AMERICANS.
2. WASPS
3. BUSINESSMEN
4. HARD-HATS
5. ETHNICS
6. JOCKS
7. ROTARIANS
8. TEXANS
9. POLICEMEN
10. SOUTHERNERS
11. SUBURBANITES
12. MILITARY MEN
13. HUNTERS
14. FLAG-WAVERS
15. STRAIGHTS
16. LILY-WHITES
17. REDNECKS
18. RED-BAITERS
19. VETERANS
20. BLUE NOSES
21. ASTRONAUTS

when it runs riot with a shotgun, Molotov cocktail or plastic bomb. Oh, do I ever react! I react to the phonies who would re-write Little Red Riding Hood to have her "rehabilitate" the wolf while screaming "hate-monger" at the woodsman coming to her rescue.

You'd better believe I'm a reactionary. In my book, it's time all responsible adults began reacting instead of suffering the insults, inconveniences and intimidations of a noisy minority who would sacrifice their own freedom—and ours—on the altar of atheistic materialism.

If the majority will just begin reacting, the kooks and the creeps would soon crawl back under their rocks, and this tired old world would have time to bind its wounds and regain its sense of humor.

**Less Government,
More Individual Responsibility
And With God's Help,
A Better World.**

From the November, 1980 issue of *Armed Citizen News*.

DISCUSSION
ACTIVITY **4**

DISTINGUISHING BETWEEN BIAS AND REASON

Governmental officials, political writers and others generally carry one of the labels of the political spectrum. These individuals are so labeled because of the opinions they hold regarding government, society and human nature. Some of these opinions are based only on feelings and others are based on facts. One of the most important critical thinking skills is the ability to distinguish between opinions based on emotions or bias and conclusions based on a rational consideration of the facts.

Some of the following statements have been taken from the viewpoints in this book and some have other origins. Consider each statement carefully. Mark *R* for any statement you feel is based on reason and a rational consideration of the facts. Mark *B* for any statement you believe is based on bias, prejudice or emotion. Mark *I* for any statement you think is impossible to judge. Then discuss and compare your judgments with other class members.

R = A Statement Based On Reason
B = A Statement Based On Bias
I = A Statement Impossible To Judge

113

_____ 1. Government is the most dangerous institution known to man. Throughout history it has violated the rights of men more than any individual or group of individuals could do.

_____ 2. Human beings want to share love, share well-being, share power and want human dignity to prevail.

_____ 3. Governments would be needed even if men were angels.

_____ 4. Men are unequal in terms of ambition, ability, intelligence and character.

_____ 5. Unions too often just represent the organized few and raise their wages so high that the unorganized many cannot find work.

_____ 6. Church-going people are more patriotic than those who do not attend church.

_____ 7. Government should assist the helpless, but only when they cannot help themselves, for to do so might destroy their individual self-respect.

_____ 8. A conservative congress and presidency would be best for the United States during the 1980's.

_____ 9. America would be much better off if it were totally rid of extremist political groups such as the American Nazi Party and the Communist Party, USA.

_____ 10. Liberals are more concerned about the welfare of others than conservatives.

_____ 11. All people are essentially political animals. That is, they need to live in social-political groupings with their fellows.

_____ 12. In a democracy, power arises from those over whom it is exercised, namely, the people. Therefore, democracy is the best form of government.

"All that which an individual posses-ses by right (including his life and property) are morally his to use, dispose of and even destroy, as he sees fit."

What Libertarianism Is

John Hospers

John Hospers is professor of philosophy at the University of Southern California. Currently a member of the Publications Board of the Libertarian Party's 1980 Presidential Committee, in 1972, he ran as the party's first presidential candidate. He is the author of several books, including *Libertarianism, Human Conduct, Introduction to Philosophical Analysis, Understanding the Arts* and the forthcoming *Will Capitalism Survive?* In the following viewpoint, he provides a basic outline of libertarian principles and of the role of laws and government in the libertarian scheme.

Consider the following questions while reading:
1. **According to Hospers, how many types of laws are there and what are those laws?**
2. **What should the role of government be?**
3. **According to Hospers, is welfare necessary? Why or why not?**
4. **Does libertarianism appear to be a workable form of government?**

The political philosophy that is called libertarianism (from the Latin *libertas*, liberty) is the doctrine that every person is the owner of his own life, and that no one is the owner of anyone else's life; and that consequently every human being has the right to act in accordance with his own choices, unless those actions infringe on the equal liberty of other human beings to act in accordance with *their* choices.

LIBERTARIAN BELIEFS

There are several other ways of stating the same libertarian thesis:

1. *No one is anyone else's master, and no one is anyone else's slave.*

Since I am the one to decide how my life is to be conducted, just as you decide about yours, I have no right (even if I had the power) to make you my slave and be your master, nor have you the right to become the master by enslaving me. Slavery is *forced* servitude, and since no one owns the life of anyone else, no one has the right to enslave another...

2. *Other men's lives are not yours to dispose of...*

A hundred men might gain great pleasure from beating up or killing just one insignificant human being; but other men's lives are not theirs to dispose of. "In order to achieve the worthy goals of the next five–year–plan, we must forcibly collectivize the peasants..."; but other men's lives are not theirs to dispose of. Do you want to occupy, rent-free, the mansion that another man has worked for twenty years to buy? But other men's lives are not yours to dispose of. Do you want operas so badly that everyone is forced to work harder to pay for their subsidization through taxes? But other men's lives are not yours to dispose of. Do you want to have free medical care at the expense of other people, whether they wish to provide it or not? But this would require them to work longer for you whether they want to or not, and other men's lives are not yours to dispose of...

3. *No human being should be a nonvoluntary mortgage on the life of another...*

All that which an individual possesses by right (including his life and property) are morally his to use, dispose of and even destroy, as he sees fit. If I own my life, then it follows that I am free to associate with whom I please and not to associate with whom I please. If I own my knowledge and services it follows that I may ask any compensation I wish for providing

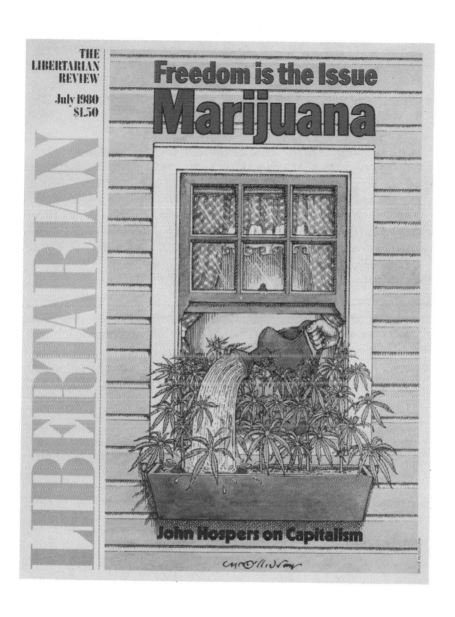

Cover of the July, 1980 issue of *The Libertarian Review*, published monthly by Libertarian Review, Inc., 1620 Montgomery Street, San Francisco, CA 94111. $12.00 per year.

them for another, or I may abstain from providing them at all, if I so choose. If I own my house, it follows that I may decorate it as I please and live in it with whom I please. If I control my own business, it follows that I may charge what I please for my products or services, hire whom I please and not hire whom I please. All that which I own in fact, I may dispose of as I choose to in reality. For anyone to attempt to limit my freedom to do so is to violate my rights...

ABOLISH GOVERNMENT

Libertarians favor the abolition of all States everywhere, and the provision of legitimate functions now supplied poorly by governments (police, courts, etc.) by means of the free market. Libertarians favor liberty as a natural human right, and advocate it not only for Americans but for all peoples. In a purely libertarian world, therefore, there would be no "foreign policy" because there would be no States, no governments with a monopoly of coercion over particular territorial areas.

Murray N. Rothbard, *For a New Liberty.*

GOVERNMENT IS DANGEROUS

Government is the most dangerous institution known to man. Throughout history it has violated the rights of men more than any individual or group of individuals could do: it has killed people, enslaved them, sent them to forced labor and concentration camps, and regularly robbed and pillaged them of the fruits of their expended labor. Unlike individual criminals, government has the power to arrest and try; unlike individual criminals, it can surround and encompass a person totally, dominating every aspect of one's life, so that one has no recourse from it but to leave the country (and in totalitarian nations even that is prohibited). Government throughout history has a much sorrier record than any individual, even that of a ruthless mass murderer. The signs we see on bumper stickers are chillingly accurate: "Beware: the Government is Armed and Dangerous..."

Government undertakes to be the individual's protector; but historically governments have gone far beyond this function. Since they already have the physical power, they have not hesitated to use it for purposes far beyond that which was entrusted to them in the first place. Undertaking initially to protect its citizens against aggression, it has often itself become an aggressor—a far greater aggressor, indeed, than the criminals against whom it was supposed to protect its citizens. Governments have done what no private citizens can do: arrest and imprison individuals without a trial and send them to slave labor camps. Government must have power in order to be effective—and yet the very means by which alone it can be effective make it vulnerable to the abuse of power, leading to managing the lives of individuals and even inflicting terror upon them...

TYPES OF LAWS

Laws may be classified into three types: (1) laws protecting individuals against themselves, such as laws against fornication and other sexual behavior, alcohol, and drugs; (2) laws protecting individuals against aggressions by other individuals, such as laws against murder, robbery, and fraud; (3) laws requiring people to help one another; for example, all laws which rob Peter to pay Paul, such as welfare.

FEAR GOVERNMENT

Government is not reason; it is not eloquence; it is force! Like fire, it is a dangerous servant and a fearful master.

George Washington

Libertarians reject the first class of laws totally. Behavior which harms no one else is strictly the individual's own affair. Thus, there should be no laws against becoming intoxicated, since whether or not to become intoxicated is the individual's own decision; but there should be laws against driving while intoxicated, since the drunken driver is a threat to every other motorist on the highway (drunken driving falls into type 2). Similarly, there should be no laws against drugs (except the prohibition of sale of drugs to minors) as long as the taking of these drugs poses no threat to anyone else. Drug addiction is a psychological problem to which no present solution exists. Most of the social harm caused by addicts, other than to themselves, is the result of thefts which they perform in order to continue their habit—and then the *legal* crime is the theft, not the addiction...

119

Laws should be limited to the second class only: aggression by individuals against other individuals. These are laws whose function is to protect human beings against encroachment by others; and this, as we have seen, is (according to libertarianism) the sole function of government.

Libertarians also reject the third class of laws totally: no one should be forced by law to help others, not even to tell them the time of day if requested, and certainly not to give them a portion of one's weekly paycheck. Governments, in the guise of humanitarianism, have given to some by taking from others (charging a "handling fee" in the process, which, because of government's waste and inefficiency, sometimes is several hundred percent). And in so doing, they have decreased incentive, violated the rights of individuals, and lowered the standard of living of almost everyone.

All such laws constitute what libertarians call *moral cannibalism*. A cannibal in the physical sense is a person who lives off the flesh of other human beings. A *moral* cannibal is one who believes he has a right to live off the "spirit" of other human beings — who believes that he has a moral claim on the productive capacity, time, and effort expended by others...

GOVERNMENTAL IDEAL

The ideal government of all reflective men, from Aristotle onward, is one which lets the individual alone — one which barely escapes being no government at all.

H. L. Mencken

Many questions, particularly about economic matters, will be generated by the libertarian account of human rights and the role of government. Should government have no role in assisting the needy, in providing social security, in legislating minimum wages, in fixing prices and putting a ceiling on rents, in curbing monopolies, in erecting tariffs, in guaranteeing jobs, in managing the money supply? To these and all similar questions the libertarian answers with an unequivocal no.

"But then you'd let people go hungry!" comes the rejoinder. This, the libertarian insists, is precisely what would not happen; with the restrictions removed, the economy would flourish as never before. With the controls taken off business, existing enterprises would expand and new ones would spring into existence satisfying more and more consumer needs; millions more people would be gainfully employed instead of subsisting on welfare, and all kinds of research and production, released from the stranglehold of government, would proliferate, fulfilling man's needs and desires as never before.

Ed Clark, 1980 Libertarian Presidential Candidate

"Libertarianism is opposed to all conservative traditions, to tradition itself."

A Conservative Reply to Libertarianism

Ernest van den Haag

Ernest van den Haag is a lecturer in psychology and sociology at the New School for Social Research and Adjunct Professor of Social Philosophy at New York University. The author of numerous books, his articles appear frequently in leading periodicals. In the following viewpoint, he compares and contrasts libertarianism and conservatism.

Consider the following questions while reading:
1. In what areas would conservatives and libertarians agree?
2. Why does van den Haag believe that libertarianism would not work?
3. Do you agree with van den Haag's criticism of libertarianism? Please discuss your answer.

Ernest van den Haag, "Libertarians and Conservatives," *National Review*, June 8, 1979. Reprinted with permission of the author.

Both libertarians and conservatives believe that only a free market can produce widespread prosperity: neither believes in vast, coercive redistributive schemes which are self-defeating—the intended beneficiaries hardly benefit—and (libertarians believe) immoral. Both believe that people are entitled to whatever they can earn in a free market; that individuals should have the right, singly or in corporate groups, to own, produce, buy, and sell whatever they wish, at whatever prices they can get, and to hire whomever they wish, at whatever wages are acceptable, with a minimum (none, for libertarians) of government regulation or monopoly. Both groups believe that economic freedom is essential not just to prosperity and efficiency but also to individual freedom...

BROAD DIFFERENCES

There is something refreshing about the libertarians' unabashed defense of the free market and their attack on government interference everywhere. Some conservatives feel that libertarianism deserves support as a perhaps exaggerated, version of their own belief in the free market—just as some liberals kept a soft spot for Communism as an exaggerated version of their own beliefs. They were wrong. So are conservatives who keep a soft spot for libertarianism. There are unbridgeable chasms on moral, political, and social issues: despite the shared belief in free markets—despite the shared opposition to big government, to excessive taxation and interference, to the restriction of our freedom in favor of a phony equality (actually of bureaucracy)—libertarian and conservative beliefs are mutually exclusive on essential matters. Libertarianism is opposed to all conservative traditions, to tradition itself. It is inconsistent with the anti-utopian conservative view of life and society.

Conservatives believe that (limited) constitutional government is essential "to secure these rights"—to life, liberty, and the pursuit of happiness. Libertarians repudiate this insight of the Founding Fathers. They oppose all government, and they repudiate the need for social cultivation of the social bond, for public authority, and for legally enforced rules. They are opposed to the Constitution and to the American heritage. Indeed, libertarians repudiate essential elements of civilization as it has historically developed everywhere...

I doubt that I would like a libertarian society, but I needn't worry, because it is wholly utopian (the word means "nowhere"). However, utopian thought can be dangerous. The desired Utopia cannot be achieved; but the destruction of an existing society may be. And it is quite likely to be succeeded by a worse one...

NEED FOR GOVERNMENT

Contrary to what James Madison thought, governments would be needed even "if men were angels." For the need for coercive authority arises not only from the wickedness of all, or of some, and from their infinite wish for power (palpable as these are); even among good men, even among angels, conflicts may arise that can be decided only by violence — unless there is a superior authority that can decide, and enforce its decision. Thus, although Ralph Nader thinks all good men are with him, some good men may feel that, in a given situation, nuclear power is better than no electricity. Other "angels" may disagree. Unless there is an authority (whether vested in a majority or in a court), force will have to decide the issue. Belief in a government authority, albeit a limited one, distinguishes conservatives, who continue to support the American Constitution and the principles underlying it, from libertarians, who reject it. Consider now a few particulars.

LIBERTARIANS AND CONSERVATIVES

Libertarianism ignores any social good unless individuals will pay for it or are willing and able to defend it.

Ernest van den Haag

Externalities. Some things, or services, are desired by most people. But the desired things cannot be so limited that only those benefit who are willing to pay. The benefits of national defense, of the education of children (if their parents cannot pay, or if they are orphans), of public parks, streets, traffic lights, police, etc. are indiscriminate and diffuse. Nobody can be excluded for not paying, and voluntary contributions will not suffice. If such things are to be provided at all they have to be paid for by taxes—which libertarians oppose...

Punishment. Libertarians believe variously that punishment for crime 1) is unneeded altogether, or 2) could be administered by private associations, or 3) could be replaced by restitution. But all libertarians believe that crime is a matter between victim and victimizer, a matter of retaliation or compensation, not an act that organized society must punish according to law, regardless of individual victims.

Those who believe in restitution alone neglect the obvious fact that, if he had to pay no more than restitution to the bereaved, a rich man would have a license to murder, and that anyone could murder or abuse those who had no chance to join protective associations—e.g., young orphans or those who have no one to whom restitution would be owed. Further, a burglar could go about his business, and pay full restitution —when caught. Since burglars are rarely caught, burglary would become even more profitable—and frequent—than it is now. What restitution does a spy owe...?

THE ABORTION QUESTION

Ingenious libertarians have tried to meet these problems. Where they have been successful, the solution remarkably resembles the institutions it was to replace. In other cases, I cannot see any solution. Consider abortion. The question is: Should the fetus have rights enforceable by society, against the rights and wishes of the mother, when the two are in conflict? One can deny the fetus the status of a human being *in spe.* But there is nothing that commits libertarians to that position. Some, indeed, oppose abortion. But they could not outlaw it in a libertarian society; nothing could be outlawed. Nor could the fetus join a private security association to protect itself, nor ask for restitution or punishment. The parents, who are responsible for its extinction, certainly won't. Who but society could protect the fetus, or babies, incompetents, and orphans? Libertarianism ignores any social good unless individuals will pay for it or are willing and able to defend it...

The idea that a crime is committed only when there is an individual victim rests on moral obtuseness and is incorrect even with regard to minor violations. Suppose one of my students cheats. There are no individual victims. (I don't grade on a curve.) Suppose he bribes me. No individual victims. Yet, I think punishment is needed, if grading is not to become so unreliable as to damage society...

AN IMPERFECT SOCIETY

The cast of American conservative thought is profoundly antiutopian. While it recognizes the continuing historical certainty of change and the necessity of basic principle being expressed under different circumstances in different ways, and while it strives always for the improvement of human institutions and the human condition, it rejects absolutely the idea that society or men generally are perfectible.

Frank S. Meyer, from his book *Conservatism.*

NECESSITY FOR LAWS

We all renounce rape, burglary, murder, and fraud because we are collectively better off that way. For this reason we try to make it costly for individuals to commit crimes. The criminal takes unfair advantage of our willingness to abstain from doing what he does. His crime does not merely harm the individual victim (if any) but all law–abiding people. Kidnapping or holding hostages on a plane harms specific victims. But even if they all were willing to forgive, or to be paid off, the kidnapper must be punished. His act endangers others besides the actual victims; it makes flying, and society, less safe. However necessary restitution to victims may be, the main issue is: Shall we all submit to law—and punish those who don't—or shall each of us provide for his own security as best he can? On this issue conservatives are for, libertarians against, law.

126

"As understood by the libertarian, man seems to be all grandeur and no misery, all Eden and no Fall."

A Liberal Reply to Libertarianism

James W. Woelfel

James W. Woelfel is professor of philosophy and religion at the University of Kansas, in Lawrence. In the following viewpoint, originally entitled "We're Not Rational Animals: A Liberal Reply to Libertarianism", the author examines libertarianism from the perspective of Christian theology and contemporary liberalism. The article has recently appeared in a book by Woelfel, *Augustinian Humanism: Essays in Human Bondage and Earthly Grace.*

Consider the following questions while reading:

1. **According to Woelfel, what is the principle flaw in libertarian thinking?**
2. **What does the author feel is the "distinctive contribution and strength" of 20th century liberalism?**
3. **Do you agree with Woelfel's criticism of libertarianism? Be able to discuss your answer.**

James W. Woelfel, "We're Not Rational Animals: A Liberal Reply to Libertarianism," *The Christian Century.* Copyright 1973 Christian Century Foundation. Reprinted by permission from the November 7, 1973 issue of *The Christian Century.*

Over the past few years I have followed with keen interest the resurgence of libertarian thought and activity in the United States. My reading began with Ayn Rand, spread to her schismatic disciple Nathaniel Branden and her distinguished philosophical convert John Hospers, and then broadened out to include the larger panoply of libertarian views represented by *Reason* magazine. Most recently I have read Murray Rothbard's *For a New Liberty* — a book that the leading libertarian at my university has compared with Marx's *Communist Manifesto* for persuasiveness and (hopefully) for historical significance...

A FLAW AT THE FOUNDATION

I must confess to being mightily stirred by libertarian literature, particularly Rothbard's sort. No group sounds the theme of individual human freedom the way the libertarians do. Libertarian criticisms of past and present governments for their arrogance and power-seeking, their everlasting meddling in people's lives and their ruthless willingness to sacrifice human beings to "public interest," their appalling war making — these strike a responsive chord in any reasonably sensitive person who has studied even our own politically advantaged country's history and participated in its life over the past ten years. Libertarians stand squarely with the most ardent civil-liberties liberals in defending Bill of Rights guarantees and in advocating a maximum of personal freedom on such issues as women's liberation, abortion, divorce, conscientious objection, censorship, victimless crimes, treatment of mental patients, and sexual relations between consenting adults...

Yet there is a flaw at the very foundation of the libertarians' edifice. They have a superficial doctrine of human existence and behavior. In biological and psychological terms, the libertarians seem only very mildly aware that human beings *qua* human beings are saddled with a heavy genetic-evolutionary, psychic and environmental burden. In the language of philosophy, they neglect the fact that human life is heavily weighted on the side of "facticity" or destiny — a destiny which, theology adds, is mysteriously distorted and broken.

The libertarian Achilles' heel is the definition of human beings as free and rational animals.... To them, the human being is uniquely the animal who can and must survive by the voluntary exercise of his individual conceptual abilities rather than by instinct. Since we cannot survive in a fully "programmed" manner like other animals, we must each exercise our rational abilities by choice, volitionally. Every normal human being, according to libertarian theoreticians, possesses this basic freedom of rational choice, whatever his or her endowments and circumstances. The assumptions of the essential rationality and sovereign freedom of the individual form the intellectual foundation of the libertarian creed and the constant theme of libertarian writings...

ARE WE RATIONAL?

The problem of freedom is intimately connected with this fact. Human beings are in some sense uniquely free, but by no means sovereignly and rationally so, as libertarians assume...

"US" AND "THEM"

Libertarianism has always been and continues to be hopelessly utopian...

Issue by issue, libertarians have offered slogans rather than realistic solutions for the problems of the day. Thus, all non-libertarians are branded "statists" or "collectivists"; all who do not believe in unadulterated laissez-faire capitalism are "socialists" or "welfare statists," including those whose basic orientation is toward a free market economy. There are no shades of grey for most libertarians. There is no room for reality, only the extreme worlds of "us" and "them."

Jerome Tuccille, Libertarian Candidate for Governor of New York in 1974.

Human freedom operates elusively and fragilely within that same formidable context of heredity and environment which obtains in the case of human rationality. Freedom seems to be much more often a hidden spontaneity directed toward irrational and transrational ends than a sovereign capacity to think and act...

Libertarians like Rothbard oddly combine devastating criticism of follies and perversities of human history with a remarkable optimism about essential human nature and the future possibilities of building a libertarian society. It scarcely seems to occur to them to wonder why, if we are such nobly

129

rational animals, we have so consistently and almost unanimously behaved in such outrageously sheeplike and nonrational ways. Committed as they are to describing human groups simply as collections of individuals and to rejecting all abstract and "mystical" notions of "state" or "government" or "society," libertarians in theory at least have no one to blame for the perversities of history but individual human beings themselves.

Yet, curiously enough, libertarians leave us with an inexplicable gap between the individual rational animal and the perversities that characterize human history, and fall into talking about government and various forms of social organizations and institutionalization as a kind of abstract "them" over against rational, productive "us." Why states and churches and various other social institutions and mythologies have tyrannized over rational individuals from time immemorial is the glaring question libertarians leave unanswered. Their problem is that if they were to grant (as they ought) that the grotesqueries of history are rooted deeply in human nature itself, then they would have to concede that we *homo saps* are neither free nor rational enough to live in a world where everything is governed only by free exchange of goods and services. They would have to grant that power–seeking on the one hand and easy subservience on the other are constants of the human condition. They might even have to admit that, given our marvelous human potentialities and our tragic human limitations, at least some kinds of government may have both a positive and a negative role to play as a terribly imperfect but needed check on the injustices arising from this peculiar mix of potentialities and limitations.

HUMANS HAVE LIMITS

The liberal needs to remind the libertarian that his principles and practices emphasize only one side of human nature — our noble possibilities as possessors of a unique measure of freedom and reason — and underplay the bondages and irrationalities resulting from our formidable natural and social limitations.

POTENTIALS AND SAFEGUARDS

Enter the liberal — or at least *my* liberal. For me, the distinctive contribution and strength of 20th century liberalism at its best lies in the uniting of passionate commitment to human potentialities with a realistic assessment of human limitations. Liberalism is more adequate than libertarianism because, taking a sober view of those aspects of human nature that determine much of the way in which we choose and reason, it recognizes the need for safeguards against their undesirable manifestations, while at the same time devoting itself to creating conditions that make for the broad realization of our possibilities as human beings.

That, so far as I am concerned, is the sum total of the liberal "creed." It is a somewhat sloppy social and political perspective, utterly lacking in the crisp consistency of libertarianism; but I believe it shows deeper understanding of our very sloppy world.

THE IMPOSSIBLE DREAM

The libertarian affirmation of individual human dignity, freedom and rationality is a refreshing and urgently needed one, coming from what is for the liberal a new and unexpected part of the political spectrum. The passionate defense of individual rights and liberties by Rothbard and other libertarians, and their vigilant criticisms of governmental arrogance and corruption, should be welcomed by liberals on most counts. But the liberal in turn needs to remind the libertarian that his principles and practices emphasize only one side of human nature — our noble possibilities as possessors of a unique measure of freedom and reason — and underplay the bondages and irrationalities resulting from our formidable natural and social limitations. In its admittedly muddled way liberalism tries to do justice to the whole perplexing mix of human potentialities and limitations which produces the ambiguities, sins and tragedies of human history.

Out of this "humane realism" comes the liberal belief that laissez-faire is not a possible state of human society; that human rights and possibilities require an active offsetting of human irrationalities. As understood by the libertarian, man seems to be all grandeur and no misery, all Eden and no Fall. Such angelism produces a social and political theory full of noble sentiment but lacking in depth and possibility.

Publications
of the Far Right

Organizations	Publications
National Association for the Advancement of White People	NAAWP News Box 10625 New Orleans, LA 70181 Published Monthly $10.00 per year
National Socialist White People's Party	White Power N.S. Publications Box 50360 Cicero, IL 60650 Published Bi-Monthly $4.00 per 12 issues
National Socialist League	N. S. Mobilizer P. O. Box 26496 Los Angeles, CA 90025 Published Semi-Annually $2.00 per year
Freedom Press	Voice of Freedom P. O. Box 24836 Dallas, TX 75224 Published Monthly $5.00 per year
The Odinist Movement	The Odinist P. O. Box 731 Adelaide St. Toronto, 210, Ontario Canada
National States Rights Party	The Thunderbolt P. O. Box 1211 Marietta, GA 30061 Published Monthly $8.00 per year

The addresses and subscription rates of these periodicals are correct as of 1980.

America's Future	America's Future
	542 Main Street
	New Rochelle, NY 10801
	Published Bi-Weekly
	$6.00 per year
The Invisible Empire Knights of the Ku Klux Klan	The Klansman
	Box 700
	Denham Springs, LA 70726
	Published Monthly
	$6.00 per year
American White Nationalist Party	Bulletin of the American White Nationalist Party
	P. O. Box 14083
	Columbus, OH 43214
	Published Bi-Monthly
	$6.00 per year
Western Guard Universal	Aryan
	Box 1197
	Buffalo, NY 14212
	Published Occasionally
National Association to Keep and Bear Arms	Armed Citizens News
	P. O. Box 78336
	Seattle, WA 98178
New Christian Crusade Church	Christian Vanguard
	P. O. Box 426
	Metairie, LA 70004
	Published Monthly
	$8.00 per year

Publications
of the Far Left

Organization	**Publication**
Communist Worker's Party USA	Worker's Viewpoint
	GPO Box 2256
	New York, NY 10116
	Published Monthly
	$13.00 per year

World View Publishers	Worker's World 46 West 21st Street New York, NY 10010 Published Weekly $10.00 per year
Spartacist League of the US	Worker's Vanguard Box 1377, GPO New York, NY 10116 Published Bi-Weekly $3.00 per year
World Socialist Party	The Western Socialist 295 Huntington Ave. Room 212 Boston, MA 02115 Published Quarterly $1.75 per year
Washington CRAP Report	Washington CRAP Report P. O. Box 10309 St. Petersburg, FL 33733 Published Monthly $12.00 per year
Workers Press	Proletariat P. O. Box 3774 Chicago, IL 60654 Published Quarterly $6.00 per year
Marxist-Leninist Party of the USA	Proletarian Internationalism M—L Publications Box 11972 Fort Dearborn Sta. Chicago, IL 60611 Published Bi-Monthly $11.00 per year
Progressive Labor Party	Progressive Labor Magazine GPO Box 808 Brooklyn, NY 11202 Published Quarterly $5.00 per year
New Solidarity International Press Service	New Solidarity 59 Temple Place Suite 654 Boston, MA 100 Issues per year $25.00 per year

Red Tide	Red Tide 46 Elhurst Highland Park, MI 48203 Published Quarterly Voluntary Contributions
The New Socialist	The New Socialist Box 18026 Denver, CO 80218 Published Quarterly $4.00 per year
Progress Books	Communist Viewpoint Bathurst St. Toronto, Canada MSV ZP6 Published Quarterly $5.00 per year
The Workers Advocate	The Workers Advocate P. O. Box 11942 Fort Dearborn Station Chicago, IL 60611 Published Monthly $12.00 per year
Spartacist Publishing Company	Women and Revolution Box 1377, GPO New York, NY 10116 Published Quarterly $2.00 per year
Spartacist Canada Publishing Association	Spartacist Box 6867, Station A Toronto, Ontario, Canada 10 Issues per year $2.00 per year

LABELING INDIVIDUALS AND ORGANIZATIONS

Although there is a danger in simplification and generalization, it can often be quite helpful to pigeonhole ideas, people, and organizations, particularly when one is trying to master new subject matter. The chart below summarizes some of the views held by individuals at various stages of the political spectrum.

FAR LEFT
- Society's good before individual good
- The goal justifies the means
- Political ideals must not be compromised
- Belief in a Communist form of government

  LIBERAL
  - Reform by moderate means
  - Expect the best of people
  - Expanded role of government in solving social problems

    CONSERVATIVE
    - Content with the present system
    - People need enlightened control
    - The fewer government programs the better

    FAR RIGHT
    - Traditional authority must be maintained
    - All laws must be observed
    - Political ideals must not be compromised
    - Communism is the root of many problems

Left 10 9 8 7 6 5 4 3 2 1 0 1 2 3 4 5 6 7 8 9 10 Right

Far Left   Liberal   Conservative   Far Right

1. Position on the spectrum the following individuals whose viewpoints appear in this chapter. Present arguments to defend your placements.

   (Example: Adolf Hitler   <u>Right 10</u>)

   Harold Freeman _____

   Patricia Young _____

   John Hospers _____

   Ernest van den Haag _____

   James J. Woelfel _____

2. List three prominent Americans who you think could be easily positioned on the left side of the political spectrum. Be able to defend your positioning.

   1. _____

   2. _____

   3. _____

   List three prominent Americans who you think could be easily positioned on the right side of the political spectrum. Be able to defend your positioning.

   1. _____

   2. _____

   3. _____

3. What national organizations and famous personalities do you think could be easily positioned on the spectrum? Which would be difficult to position? Be able to give your reasons in each instance.

4. Some people claim the political spectrum should be diagramed as a circle rather than as a straight line. Whereas liberals and conservatives share little mutual ground, extremists of the far right and left have many things in common. What merit do you see in this idea?

HELPFUL PERIODICAL ARTICLES

The editors have compiled a bibliography of helpful and recent periodicals. The majority of the periodicals listed below are available in most school and public libraries. We encourage students to read some of the articles in order to broaden their knowledge of the political spectrum.

THE POLITICAL SPECTRUM

Commentary	*What Is a Liberal — Who Is a Conservative?*, September 1976, p. 31. (a number of journalists attempt to answer the above question).
Henry Fairlie	*Galloping Toward Dead Center*, **The New Republic**, 8 April 1978, p. 18.
W. L. Fieldhouse	*An Essay on Political Ignorance*, **The American**, January 1979, p. 13. (explains the difficulties in interpreting the political spectrum).
Joseph C. Harsch	*The Decline of the Left?*, **The Christian Science Monitor**, 26 October 1976, p. 35.
John Holm & John Robinson	*Ideological Voting is Alive and Well*, **Public Opinion**, April/May 1980, p. 52. (article includes excellent differentiation of liberals and conservatives).
Everett Carll Ladd, Jr.	*The New Division in U. S. Politics*, **Fortune**, 26 March 1979, p. 89.
Time	*The Trouble with Being in the Middle*, 1 July 1974, p. 18.

LIBERALISM

Reo M. Christenson	*The Liberals' Golden Oldies*, **The Christian Science Monitor**, 20 October 1980.
Commonweal	*Could Conservatives Conserve?*, 17 December 1976, p. 804.
Commonweal	*Paths to a New Liberalism*, 5 December 1980, p. 675.
Anne Higgins	*The Hassle of Being Liberal*, **National Catholic Reporter**, 12 October 1978, P. 8.

William B. Hixson, Jr.	*Liberal Legacy, Radical Critique,* **Commonweal,** 13 October 1978, p. 647 (examines the question: Are liberal principles at the root of America's current difficulties?).
The Humanist	*Liberals Vs Radicals: Is There a Radical Difference,* July/August 1970, p. 7.
Roberta Lynch	*Strong Negatives in the Decline of Liberalism in the U.S.,* **In These Times,** 6 September 1977.
George W. Shannon	*Liberal Whites of 1960's Leery of Integration,* **Manchester Union Leader,** 22 April 1980, p. 20.
Glenn Tinder	*Liberals and Revolution,* **The New Republic,** 27 January 1979, p. 21.
Alan Tonelson	*Bring Back Hell Fire,* **The New Republic,** 26 February 1977, p. 18. (liberals argue for reform on the basis of self-interest).

CONSERVATISM

John B. Anderson	*How to Identify True Conservatives,* **The Minneapolis Tribune,** 7 December 1980.
Peter L. Berger	*Two Paradoxes,* **National Review,** 12 May 1972. p. 507. (Berger contends that there are two paradoxes in conservatism).
Robert C. Byrd	*In Defense of Conservatism,* **New Guard,** March 1972, p. 11.
Conservative Digest	*The New Right: A Special Report,* June 1979, p. 9.
Clarence B. Carson	*The Property Basis of Rights,* **The Freeman,** September 1980, p. 543.
Amitai Etzioni	*A Swing to the Right?* **Trans-Action,** September 1970, p. 12.
M. Stanton Evans	*The Conservative Mainstream,* **National Review,** 31 October 1980, p. 1326.
Edwin Feulner	*Conservative Rebels,* **Conservative Digest,** March 1980, p. 16. (a corps of young conservative thinkers challenging traditional liberal dogmas).
George Gilder	*Ex-Neoconservative Praises the New Right for Common Sense Stands on the Issues,* **Conservative Digest,** September 1980, p.34.
John Judis	*The Right May Be Wrong, but the Left Isn't Right,* **The Progressive,** August 1979, p. 22.

Irving Kristol	*Confessions of a True, Self-Confessed — Perhaps the Only — Neoconservative,* **Public Opinion,** October/November 1979, p.50.
Suzannah Lessard	*The Real Conservatism,* **The Washington Monthly,** July/August 1973.
John D. Lofton, Jr.	*Left Using Smear Tactics,* **The Manchester Union Leader,** 2 October 1980.
George F. Will	*The Maturing of U. S. Conservatives,* **The Minneapolis Tribune,** 13 November 1980.
Walter E. Williams	*What's Wrong with Turning Back the Clock?,* **The Manchester Union Leader,** 25 September 1980.

EXTREMISM

Alan Brownfeld	*Collectivism: The Common Root of Nazism, Communism and Socialism,* **Manchester Union Leader,** 15 May 1980, p. 26.
John Judis	*Libertarianism: Where the Left Meets the Right,* **The Progressive,** September 1980, p. 36.
Charlene Mitchell	*A Strategy to Defeat the Ultra-Right,* **Daily World,** 8 May 1980, p. 12. (Charlene Mitchell is a member of the political bureau, Communist Party USA).
The People	*Libertarianism: Reaction in Disguise,* 4 October 1980, p. 5.
Peter Schrag	*America's Other Radicals,* **Harpers,** August 1970, p. 35. (an article discussing the influence in America of the political far right).
Joseph Sobran	*In Praise of Libertarianism,* **St. Paul Pioneer Press,** 16 August 1979.
Time	*An Elegy for the New Left,* 15 August 1977, p. 67.
George Vickers	*A Guide to the Sectarian Left,* **The Nation,** 17 May 1980, p. 591.
Dale Vree	*A Fascism in Our Future?* **Worldview,** November 1977, p. 14.

Index

abortion, 125, 128
Aid to Families with Dependent
  Children, 53
anarchy, 31
Anderson, John, 63

Beveridge, Albert, 32
Burke, Edmund, 26, 30-31, 34

capitalism, 24, 43, 50, 77-78, 102,
  106-108, 129
censorship, 42
civil liberties, 21, 22, 83, 102, 128,
  civil rights, 56, 58, civil service, 26
Clark, Ed, 101
communism, 103, 123, communist,
  34-35, 90, 102, 104, 110, anti-
  communist, 57, 102

democracy, 29, 45, 65, 90, 108,
  American democracy, 88, participatory democracy, 104
democratic government, 24, 88, 92,
  party (Democrats), 32, 48,
  democratic principle, 108
detente, 88
Disraeli, Benjamin, 34

economic, 25, 26, 31, 61, 62, 64, 76,
  88, 91, 106, 120, economic environment, 25, economic equality,
  72, economic floor, 90, economic

freedom, 76-79, 81, 82, 123,
  economic isolationism, 35,
  economic liberties, 21-22, economic order, 42, economic realities, 86, economic reform, 90
  economic system, 50, 92
economy, 32, 34, 46, 57, 65, 78, 106,
  120, 129
egalitarianism, 84, 86, 90
environment, 24-25, 107, 129,
  environmental, 53, 128
equality, 25-27, 31, 42, 72, 78, 82,
  84, 86, 88, 90, 92, 107-108, 123,
  equal rights, 30, 56
established order, 26
extremist, 19, 99-104

fascist, 22, 34, 110
federalists, 32
Founding Fathers, 30, 81, 123
Fourteenth Amendment, 32
Frankfurter, Felix, 83
free enterprise, 26, 81, 83, 121, 129,
  free market, 77-78, 118, 123, 129,
  private enterprise 58

Great Society, 57, 58, 85

Hamilton, Alexander, 28, 32
Hospers, John, 128, viewpoint, 115-
  121
Hoover, Herbert, 35

House of Representatives, 19

indoctrinating, 25
inequality, 26-27, 108
inflation, 61-63, 65
integration, 50
internationalist, 35
isolationism, 88, isolationist, 35

Jefferson, Thomas, 29-30, 32

Kennedy, Edward M., 29
Kennedy, John F., 54, 62, 64
Kristol, Irving, 90, viewpoint, 84-88

leftist, 19-20, 21-22, 103, radical, 19-20, 61, 91, 110
libertarianism, 101, 115-120, 122-126, 127, libertarian, 22, 115-120, 123-126, 127
liberty, 22, 26-27, 29, 31, 83, 88, 90, 116-118, 123
Lincoln, Abraham, 30

McGovern, George, 46
Madison, James, 122, 124
Marx, Karl, 23-24, 107-108, 128
Mill, John Stuart, 30
minorities, 30
moderate, 22
monarchy, 30-31, 74
monetary system, 63

Nader, Ralph, 124
National Conservative Political
Action Committee, 29
nationalists, 32
natural law, 26, natural man, 24
Nazism, 45
neo-conservatism, 84-88, 89-92
New Deal, 35, 58
New Frontier, 90
nihilism, 86
Nixon, Richard, 63

one-world order, 25

Peace Corps, 57
popular sovereignty, 24
populism, 92
private property, 24, 27, 74, 81-83, 107, 116-118
progressive, 24, 45

radical, (see leftist)
reactionary, (see rightist)
Reagan, Ronald, 58, 60
Republican Party, 32, 48
revolution, 19, 25, 110, Industrial
revolution, 26
rightist, 19-20, 21-22, 102, reaction-ary, 19-20, 56, 109-110, 112
Roosevelt, Franklin D., 20, 30, 48, 81, 103
Roosevelt, Theodore, 32
Root, Elihu, 32
Rothbard, Murray N., 118, 128-129, 131
Rousseau, Jean Jacques, 23-24

secularism, 43
self reliance, 26
Senate, 19
Shaw, George Bernard, 25
socialism, 22, 25, 91, 102, 103, 105-108, socialist, 50, 107, 129, Fabian
Socialists, 25
Soviet Union, 35, 61, Soviet Jews, 90
Spencer, Herbert, 30-31
suffrage, 42

Taft, William Howard, 32
tax, 61, 65, 82, 116, 123, 125
totalitarian, 22, 77, 118
Tugwell, Rexford, 20

Utopian (Utopia), 25, 74, 123, 129

welfare, 49, 53, 85-85, 91, 103, 110, 119, 129
Wilson, Woodrow, 32
working class (workers), 24-25, 106

MEET
THE
EDITORS

David L. Bender is a history graduate from the University of Minnesota. He also has an M.A. in government from St. Mary's University in San Antonio, Texas. He has taught social problems at the high school level for several years. He is the general editor of the Opposing Viewpoints Series and has authored most of the titles in the series.

Bruno Leone received his B.A. (Phi Kappa Phi) from Arizona State University and his M.A. in history from the University of Minnesota. A Woodrow Wilson Fellow (1967), he is currently an instructor at Minneapolis Community College, Minneapolis, Minnesota, where he has taught history, anthropology, and political science. In 1974-75, he was awarded a Fellowship by the National Endowment for the Humanities to research the intellectual origins of American Democracy.